Chris
Best Wishes

Postive Mind Set - Special Mind Set

Milt Theodosatos

AuthorHouse™
1663 Liberty Drive, Suite 200
Bloomington, IN 47403
www.authorhouse.com
Phone: 1-800-839-8640

© *2008 Milt Theodosatos. All rights reserved.*

No part of this book may be reproduced, stored in a retrieval system, or transmitted by any means without the written permission of the author.

First published by AuthorHouse 8/15/2008

ISBN: 978-1-4343-7321-2 (sc)

Printed in the United States of America
Bloomington, Indiana

This book is printed on acid-free paper.

This book is dedicated to my father
George Miltiadis Theodosatos.

He was my first teacher.

He was teaching me to be SPECIAL MIND SET and I did not even know it.

Contents

About the Author	Milt Theodosatos	ix
Why Another Book on MIND SET and How This Book Can Help You!		xiii
I Am Not a Doctor of Psychology		xv
Acknowledgements		xvii
Chapter 1	A Program You Can Teach Yourself!	1
Chapter 2	Weakness…Our #1 Challenge	18
Chapter 3	The Facts of Life	29
Chapter 4	Communication…The Big C	42
Chapter 5	Don't Worry About the Things We Have No Control Over-	60
Chapter 6	Don't Allow the Elements To Affect Your Performance in A Negative Way-	64
Chapter 7	Challenges and Solutions-	70
Chapter 8	God and the Devil	76
Chapter 9	Commitment and trust-	83
Chapter 10	Great Examples of POSITIVE MIND SET or NEGATIVE MIND SET	91
Chapter 11	Competitors are Made Not Born- and Overcoming the Fear of Failure	108
Chapter 12	Expectations	117
Chapter 13	The Football Bible	126
Chapter 14	Developing a Simple program	166

About the Author
Milt Theodosatos

Theodosatos was born in 1937and raised in New York City. He lived on 135th Street between Broadway and Riverside Drive in a section called Harlem. He was a white boy living in a black neighborhood which later became also known as a Spanish neighborhood. Except in those days they didn't say black or Spanish or Hispanic or Latino. The word used for black was colored and words used for Latinos was the origin of their country. Cuba, Puerto Rico, Brazil, Argentina etc.

He was educated in the New York City school system through his sophomore year where he attended George Washington High School up in Washington Heights. Going into his junior year in high school, he and his parents moved to Long Island and "Theo" attended Mineola High School where he graduated in 1955.

Theodosatos went on to Springfield College in Springfield, Massachusetts, and graduated with a Bachelor of Science degree in 1959. He went onto teach and coach in high schools for 31 years. After retiring from teaching, he continued coaching football for 16 more years.

As a football coach, "Theo" has been labeled the "rebuilder" for taking over losing programs and turning them into contenders, winners and Champions.

He has coached for forty-seven years. Forty-Two years he served as a head coach.

He has had fifteen coaching stops along the way. He has had teaching and or coaching stints in New York, New Jersey, Oklahoma, Alabama, New Hampshire, Texas and Luebeck, Germany.

While teaching and coaching, "Theo" found it necessary to try and earn extra income from outside sources to supplement his teaching and coaching salary. Thus he had four years experience in sales, insurance and the securities industry. His wife of 50 years, Georgia and he ran an antique business for 25 years.

Theodosatos, in the twi-light of his career, then moved on to the professional level of coaching football in the arena2 league. He has served as assistant head coach for the Tennessee Valley Vipers in 2003 and 2004 as well as the Rio Grande Valley Dorados of Southern Texas in 2005.

In 2006 he was called upon once again to rebuild yet another program.This time it was a program close to his heart….. to serve as head coach of the Tennessee Valley Vipers in the arena2 Professional Indoor League.

Theodosatos has been blessed with great success both as a teacher and a coach. He is the only coach in the State of New Jersey that has brought 5 different programs to the State Playoffs. His 1976 Plainfield High School team was the first high school team to play in Giants Stadium and WIN in the State Playoffs!

"Theo" coached the victorious New Jersey All Star squad in the 2000 Governors Bowl against New York State. Theodosatos has also coached baseball, basketball and track and earned nine Coach of the Year honors in 3 sports (5 in football).

One of the great honors that "Theo" has received was his selection into the New Jersey Football Coaches Hall of Fame.

"Theo's" accomplishments in coaching are like a Who's Who in Coaching. Theodosatos has spoken at dozens of clinics throughout the eastern seaboard. His favorite topics are "Motivation" and "Developing Positive Mind Set".

Theodosatos and Georgia, his wife of 50 years, reside in Huntsville, Alabama.

Why Another Book on MIND SET and How This Book Can Help You!

If you are someone who wants to become a better CEO, a better Coach, a better Leader…… If you are a person who wants to be a better parent or friend or partner, or if you are just a regular person who wants to make yourself better. If you are a person who wants to make a *difference* in life, this book can present information to you that may be *different* from the ordinary books on the subject of self-improvement…. Information that I have learned over the last 70 years. I try to explain the ideas that I call concepts, in everyday language that should be easy to understand.

Much of the information is common sense and information that all of us *may* know. The difference here is that instead of the information being in the back of our minds, I bring the information TO THE FRONT, so to speak. I try to put the information into concepts that the reader can remember and use on a daily basis. I try to create TOOLS that are easy to remember and easy to use.

I taught these concepts to all my football teams and other students when I was a teacher. I also taught these concepts in professional football. I have had the pleasure to speak to business groups, sales organizations, civic groups, religious groups, students, sport teams and others and every time my Goal was to introduce (teach) these concepts to them also.

You, the reader can use these concepts for your own IMPROVEMENT or you can use the concepts in teaching your children a POSITIVE MIND SET…SPECIAL MIND SET.

If you are a CEO, a teacher, a coach, a supervisor of any type, you can teach these concepts to the people under your supervision and leadership. I have friends all over America and in Germany who are constantly contacting me about these concepts and the importance to them in their daily lives, both personally and professionally.

I have learned much from the business world, especially the sales industry.

Taking all of this information and knowledge and adding it to my personal life experiences, I in turn developed this program of concepts. I have had so many people encourage me to write a book. Thus, this attempt at making this program available to others.

I Am Not a Doctor of Psychology

But, I do believe I have my Doctorate in Living. After 70 years of life experiences…starting with my days on the streets of New York City….to my 47 years of coaching…to my dealing from a position of leadership for 42 years….to having to deal with thousands of decisions in regards to communicating with other people such as teachers, coaches, administrators, parents, school board members, fans, the media and students, etc.,etc.

Aristotle, Plato, Socrates and Confucius never got their degree in psychology. They used their life experiences plus logic and common sense to develop ideas that were a positive force to many people throughout the ages.

Hopefully this Book with give you, the reader a FRESH insight into MIND SET that you may NOT be aware of. Hopefully, this book will be informative and FUN to read.

Acknowledgements

It is important to me to try to acknowledge as many of the people that I can remember, who through the years influenced my development of this POSITIVE MIND SET…SPECIAL MIND SET PROGRAM.

It became evident to me from the very start of my career that MIND SET of the athletes in my charge, was going to play a key role in any success we would have. Thus I could see a NEED for some type of program to work on the minds of my players.

As the years went on, I took over losing programs and became known as the "rebuilder." All of these losing programs had the same cancer. NEGATIVITY…NEGATIVITY…NEGATIVITY

It was obvious to me that before we were to win a game….. before we were to step on the field…we would have to work on MIND SET.

Starting with my first experiences of self-help......I read the great football coaches....namely; Paul "Bear" Bryant, Bud Wilkinson, Bobby Dodd, Vince Lombardi, Chuck Mather, Paul Brown, Jake Gaither, etc., etc.,.

Through the years I have attended football clinics, college spring practices, professional football pre-season camps, and have learned from some of the greatest coaches the game has ever produced. But, two coaches and their profound statements…..influenced me most through the years.

Vince Lombardi, the legendary coach of the Green Bay Packers said… "We don't coach football….we coach PEOPLE."

Jake Gaither, the legendary Florida A&M University coach said; "Football is not about X's and O's….football is about Billys and Joes." In other words….it is all about PEOPLE.

Thus, I learned that it was going to be PEOPLE SKILLS that would be the reason for any success I would have in the future.

I knew that I would have to learn from others besides football coaches. Thus, I read Dale Carnegie, Norman Vincent Peale and anything I could get my hands on. I read the Bible, Aristotle, Plato, Confucius, Buddha and right up to modern day Anthony Robbins.

Chapter 1
A Program You Can Teach Yourself!

How about that? A simple program you can teach yourself. Just read on and use the information to help make yourself a more *Positive* person and in return have a *happier* life and a chance to be *more successful* in whatever you do. *Better relationships* with loved ones…..friends at work….a better chance to advance in the career of your choosing. Learn how to overcome the *Negativity* of society….…create better *mental* health and thus have better *physical* health.

This program has taken 47 years to develop. It started when I first started teaching and coaching high school football back in 1959.

As the years went by, I changed teaching and coaching positions hoping to improve my situation. By accident I became know as a "Rebuilder" of losing programs. I say by accident because this wasn't the plan. It just happened. It was easier getting jobs at schools that had losing programs. Very few coaches wanted these positions…these jobs were treated like the plague.

With some luck and hard work, We were able to take these losing programs and turn them around into competitors, winners and even Champions. Thus I became known as "The Builder". I say WE because you can't do it alone. A coach needs players and assistant coaches who are dedicated to the concept; *" get it done".*

As the years went by, I started to get calls from Athletic Directors, Administrators and School Board members, to come to their school and bring them a WINNER.

At each position (I have coached at 18 different stops)....the attitude was the same NEGATIVE force. The same cancer was present. All I heard was that a particular school could NOT win! I heard all the excuses that you can imagine. Thus it became obvious that I was going to have to develop some kind of MIND SET for myself and in turn, transfer my MIND SET to the coaches and players and parents and administrators that I would come in contact with. It was a tall order but it had to be done.

I read everything I could get my hands on about MIND SET. I read every coaching book I could find to try and find out how successful coaches talked to their teams about attitude, etc.,etc.

My first influences were by the legendary coaches Paul "Bear" Bryant and Vince Lombardi. Coach Bryant was the great coach from the University of Alabama and Lombardi was the National Football League Legend with the Green Bay Packers.

Later I studied Norman Vincent Peale, Dale Carnegie amongst others, all the way up to modern day information by Anthony Robbins.

Thus, I was able to put together this program. A program that stresses CONCEPTS. I hope you enjoy this effort on my part. This program has been very good to me and it sure has helped the people that I have had the pleasure of working with.

Through the years I have had the opportunity to counsel students, teachers, coaches, parents and even civic and business organizations. I have had opportunity to try and help people in their marital relationships. My wife, Georgia and I have been married for 50 years. So many of my coaches have been married, twice or three times. Personal relationship problems between husbands and wives….parents and their children are a great opportunity to help people with POSITIVE MIND SET concepts. I have been blessed to be able to help people.

Concepts-

Throughout this book I will use the word CONCEPT. I try to use this word to stress an idea that I think is worth remembering in order to develop POSITIVE….SPECIAL MIND SET. Remembering these CONCEPTS will help to remember what it takes to have a BETTER MIND SET.

Information-

In writing this book and trying to explain this program, my decision is to present information that I think is necessary to understand how and why I believe we develop a NEGATIVE or POSITIVE MIND SET……an AVERAGE or SPECIAL MIND SET.

By giving you information first, and then referring to the information….specific statements…..you will understand the points that I try to make. Much of the following information is needed in order to fully comprehend what I mean by NEGATIVE or POSITIVE MIND SET…AVERAGE or SPECIAL MIND SET.

Let's start!

Food…..Positive and Negative

Let's first start off by talking about food. Food?

I thought this was about developing a more positive mind set. Well….yes, we must first talk about food. We all need food and we all eat food. If you're like me, you probably eat many foods that we could do without. You know…….those big calorie foods. But, our body needs food. Well…..guess what? Our MIND ALSO NEEDS FOOD. And we get plenty of MIND FOOD everyday. Unfortunately much of the MIND FOOD we get is what I call NEGATIVE FORCE.

Let me tell you a quick story. When I was a kid and TV first came out (1950 for us folks) ....the news was a live 15 minute program. Then News became a 30 minute program. Then News became a 1 hour program. Then 2 hours. And today News Programs are 24 hours. And what do we see and hear on the news? Mostly NEGATIVE news.

Reports about Wars....killings...robberies....rapes.... politicians cheating ...fires......over and over and over again our MIND is FED NEGATIVE FORCE. Slipped in are some nice pleasant news articles.....but very few. So our brain gets a tremendous amount of NEGATIVE FOOD. This really has a tremendous affect on us without us really being aware of it.

This pounding of NEGATIVE FORCE takes its toll on all of us. So much so that so many people we see and work with on a daily basis are negative. They are negative in how they act....what they say......and how they affect all of us.

Did you ever notice how great it is to be around a pleasant POSITIVE person? We gravitate towards that person. We like being around that person.

Are you that type of person that people like being around?????

So, I started you off on developing POSITIVE MIND SET. You now are aware of POSITIVE FORCE and NEGATIVE FORCE.

Good!

POSITVE and NEGATIVE FORCE can be called CONCEPTS that should be remembered for further discussion.

Now let's talk about point number 2.

Average and Special Mind Set and the 90-10 Rule!

Here I will introduce a concept I will call…..AVERAGE MIND SET and SPECIAL MIND SET. Also I will introduce what I call the *90-10 rule*! Meaning that 90% of the people are in an AVERAGE MIND SET mode most of the time.

These are good people…friends…relatives….people we respect….but they think average 90% of the time. Only 10% of the people are SPECIAL MIND SET most of the time. The key word is MOST of the time.

Sometimes AVERAGE MIND SET people think special and sometimes SPECIAL MIND SET people think average. Now what is all of this mumo-jumbo????

Please understand that in this world there are people who are cynical and may say….."These are head games". I say, "Baloney."

Everything we do is a head game and the quicker we realize it the quicker we will improve our relationships. The quicker we will be more successful. The quicker we will acquire better mental health.

What is AVERAGE MIND SET?

To describe Average Mind Set behavior fully could take volumes and volumes of examples. This book will give several examples and I will explain some of the differences between types of behavior which can be described as Average or Special Mind Set. Let me give just one example at this time…..about AVERAGE MIND SET.

AVERAGE MIND SET behavior is when a person worries about things they have NO control of.

Example….the weather. People worry and complain about the weather. These same people have no control over the weather. Why waste time and precious energy worrying about the weather? People will actually get sick over worry about things *they have NO control of.* We are in a SPECIAL MIND SET mode when we have learned to NOT worry about the weather BECAUSE WE HAVE NO CONTROL OVER THE WEATHER. We have learned it is a waste of time and energy worrying about the weather. We are in a SPECIAL MIND SET mode when we have learned to ONLY worry about the things we do HAVE CONTROL OF.

This is a very simple example but for the sake of explaining a difference between AVERAGE and SPECIAL MIND SET….this example will do for now.

Another concept worth remembering.........

ALWAYS REMEMBER WHAT YOUR GOAL IS......in whatever you do.

So often people forget about their goals and why they do what they do. They lose focus on what is really important and what is NOT very important.

I will refer to this Concept from time to time. ALWAYS REMEMBER WHAT YOUR GOAL IS! Everything has to do with our MIND......yes....our HEAD.

Iceberg Theory of Thinking and the 3 Major Families of the World-

Years ago I heard a man talk about Personal Development and he introduced me to the "Iceberg theory of Thinking" and The 3 Major Families of the World. It was back in 1960 and I am sorry to say that I do not remember the man's name thus I can not give him credit....his just due.

First, let's talk about the

ICEBERG THEORY OF THINKING.

He said and I am paraphrasing, since 75% of an Iceberg is usually under water, he asked us...."How is the only way you can see what is at the bottom of the Iceberg?" Naturally people responded that we would have to go under the water to the bottom to see what is there. He continued……"Yes….. but most people think on top of the water" "Sometimes to go under the water to try to understand our behavior…. well…this can be painful"

Many times, people will avoid going under the water to *truly* understand their behavior. The purpose of introducing the above information is because as we move along I will refer to; AVERAGE AND SPECIAL MIND SET….and 'GO UNDER THE WATER" referring to the Iceberg Theory of Thinking.

When we are in an AVERAGE MIND SET mode we think on top of the water. When we are in a SPECIAL MIND SET mode, we get under the water and to the truth.

Through the years, on many occasions I would ask a question of a person and that person would simply say….."I don't know." **I don't know** is not acceptable. The person is avoiding THINKING. I would always say to the person….."Give me an answer….any answer."

"I don't care what the answer is…just THINK……go under the water and give me an answer…any answer."

AVERAGE MIND SET try to avoid giving an answer that might be incorrect. To give an incorrect answer might be embarrassing. Thus it is easier and more comfortable to avoid giving an answer and the person simply says, "I don't know.". The person is really saying……

LEAVE ME ALONE…..ASK SOMEONE ELSE….DON'T BOTHER ME.

Or the person MAY TRUTHFULLY NOT KNOW the answer to the question. Regardless……I would always try to get the person UNDER THE WATER and to THINK. Come up with an answer instead of avoiding the challenge.

His second story was about the 3 Major Families of the World.

The largest family of the world is the WISHMORE family.

We all start off as WISHMORES.

Remember when we were kids…..we wished we had this…. we wished we could do that…etc, etc. WISHMORES are knee deep in AVERAGE MIND SET and never get off their butt to make their WISHES HAPPEN. Unfortunately some people stay WISHMORES their entire life. This is AVERAGE MIND SET all the way!

The second largest family of the world is the DOMORE family. We start off as WISHMORES then we get off our butt and DOMORE. We go to school….get an education…. join the service…whatever. We develop ourselves. We DO MORE! When we are DOING MORE we are in a SPECIAL MIND SET mode.

The third family of the world…the smallest family of the world is the HAVEMORE FAMILY. They HAVE MORE.

They HAVE MORE material things but more importantly they have something else that is more important than material things. They have more self-esteem…..more self-confidence. They have that SPECIAL MIND SET…..A POSITIVE MIND SET…..to take on bigger challenges with the possibility of bigger rewards. If they fail….they fail high.

AVERAGE MIND SET people think about material things when they think about becoming a HAVEMORE. The real HAVEMORE person is more interested in POSITIVE …..SPECIAL MIND SET things rather than material things. Material things are *just things*. These material things can be replaced or lost. It is the SPECIAL MIND SET things that make a difference in life. It is SPECIAL MIND SET things that separate winning from losing….ultimate success or ultimate failure.

So now everyone should be heads up to

- POSITIVE and NEGATIVE FORCE

- AVERAGE and SPECIAL MIND SET

- The ICEBERG THEORY OF THINKING

- The 3 Major Families of the World …and

- The 90-10 Rule.

Hopefully, this information and the way I present it, will help when you read on in this book because I will continuously refer to these concepts. Remember, your goal is to make yourself a POSITIVE MIND SET ....SPECIAL MIND SET PERSON.

Average or Special Things....

Now a big question....one of many.

In order to be a SPECIAL MIND SET person, do you have to do AVERAGE things or SPECIAL things? Hopefully you will answer that you have to do SPECIAL things. Now, WHAT ARE THEY?

Let's take a personal relationship for an example. Let's take your relationship with your spouse or spouse to be. If that's not a good example let's take your place of employment... your job (your supervisor).

Remember....what is your Goal?

Your Goal is to make this relationship better....more successful! On a normal day you interact with this person in many ways. Much of how you act is normal behavior. How can you improve your behavior with this person? How can you do SPECIAL things to improve your relationship with this person?

In order to be SPECIAL.....you have to do SPECIAL things. Anyone can do AVERAGE things but the SPECIAL MIND SET person will be SPECIAL by what they do...how they act…..what they say. Make a list of the different ways you can act to be SPECIAL with that person.

First of all, eliminate any NEGATIVE behavior. Let me give you an example;

A young man is unemployed. He has been looking for a job for weeks but with no luck. Then one day he finds an opportunity to work as a trainee as a salesperson for an insurance company. When he gets home that night he tells his wife about his new job. The wife is excited but she is quick to remind him that he never sold anything in his whole life. She says that it will be very difficult to sell insurance. She loves her husband and does not realize that she is feeding him NEGATIVE FORCE. She is actually discouraging her husband. She is *taking* this opportunity AWAY from him.

Is this what he really wanted to hear? His wife is *doubting* his ability and potential success. Instead, his loving wife could have reinforced him. She could have said, "What a great opportunity" "You have never sold before but you have a great personality and can learn to sell" "I believe in you….. you can do it" Or some other words to this affect.

She could have been POSITIVE…..she could have given him POSITIVE FOOD…POSITIVE FORCE. The lesson learned here is that in order to be SPECIAL MIND SET….one has to use POSITIVE FORCE and eliminate NEGATIVE FORCE. POSITIVE MIND SET and SPECIAL MIND SET are actually one and the same. NEGATIVE MIND SET is too often the same as AVERAGE MIND SET.

Weakness and Strength-

Let's talk about WEAKNESS and STRENGTH.

Unfortunately AVERAGE MIND SET is usually loaded with negative thinking which is characteristic of WEAKNESS.

SPECIAL MIND SET.....POSITIVE MIND SET.....is loaded with *Positive* Force behavior that can be classified as STRENGTH.

Clarification

Just for the record, when I am talking about SPECIAL, I am talking about being SPECIAL in a *GOOD WAY.* A person can be SPECIAL in a BAD WAY but I am not referring to this type of behavior when I say SPECIAL MIND SET.

Let me share with you a great example of a person who was SPECIAL but in a NEGATIVE way. His name was Willie Sutton. Sutton was a safe cracker....a bank robber, back in the late 1940's early 1950's. He would select Banks and at night or in the wee hours of the morning, break into the Bank and BREAK into the Bank's safe.

If there was a Bank Safe that was suppose to be impossible to BREAK into, that inspired ole Willie. There wasn't a Bank that he couldn't crack. He was on the FBI's Top 10 Most Wanted List. He never used a weapon. He always worked alone. He was caught twice and twice he was able to escape from jail. He eventually got caught a third time and he died in prison at an old age.

This was a VERY SPECIAL MIND SET man. Unfortunately, he was SPECIAL in a WRONG way.

Some people will say that we are ***all born special.*** Yes….this is true….we are all born special……no two people are the same….even identical twins have their differences. But let me make this clarification…..I am talking about behavior and MIND SET. Let's move on.

Chapter 2
Weakness...Our #1 Challenge

Prejudice and Discrimination and Labels-

One of the biggest weaknesses of our society is Prejudice and Discrimination.

Prejudice being the negative MIND SET that one class of people is better or worse than an other class of people.

Discrimination being the negative behavior *against* that class of people.

These two negative forces are the highest level of weakness in our society in this person's mind. We live in a society where everyone has to have a label. A label based on race, religion, nationality or whatever. Where is there a book that says we have to do this? Of course, there is no book... but for sure....this happens all around us. I identify this as WEAKNESS......NEGATIVE MIND SET......more often than not a characteristic of AVERAGE MIND SET.

When a member of society has to PUT PEOPLE DOWN based on race, religion or nationality, or whatever......instead of a judgment based on character and performance....then I classify this as WEAKNESS. Some people can give me an argument about these thoughts and we could talk about it all day, but for explanation sake and to try and explain what I am driving at, I call this behavior......prejudice and discrimination....

WEAKNESS.

While in college....it seems like a hundred years ago. I was in sociology class and I was reading our text about **racial prejudice** and how it existed at one time in our **country**. The chapter I was reading was discussing the State of North Carolina which used to have a rule or law, that when you registered to vote you had to write down your RACE. The application for voting mentioned that if you were one-quarter non-white, you had to put down that non-white part of you as your RACE. WOW!

How can a person be only one-quarter of something and be considered a whole of that one-quarter? I do not know if I am explaining myself properly, but let me give another example.

If a person was one-quarter black and three-quarters white, that person had to register as a black. How ridiculous!

I always thought to myself.....if a person was one-quarter Japanese and three-quarters Black.....what would they have to put down on the paper? Japanese when they were mostly Black?....WOW!

Again.......WEAKNESS...NEGATIVE FORCE.

I grew up in New York City in a section called Harlem. We had many people who were mixed blood....black and white. We didn't say black in those days....the word *colored* was used. The mixed blood people were called mulatos. Today, you never hear that word. What is wrong with it? Why can't a person be a mulato? If a person is a mulato they should be proud of it. But, today it is NOT POLITICALLY CORRECT to use that expression, I guess.

This is Ridiculous.......This is WEAKNESS.....simply put!

How can a person be BLACK if they are half white? SPECIAL MIND SET thinking would say..."I am both black and white and proud of it."

I worked one year with the American Indians in Oklahoma. I came to understand that many had the usual Indian physical characteristics that we come to expect. But, many looked just like me and were loaded with white blood. This made me understand that in our country, especially the south and southwest; many people have Indian blood and do not realize it.

No big deal!

But this was an observation I thought worth mentioning because of the need for people in our country to use labels.... and the weakness of labels.

The same can be said for the labels Liberal and Conservative. How can anyone be a total Liberal or a total Conservative?

Impossible!!!!!

We are all liberal about some things and we are all conservative about some things. Just another example of how we people have been programmed to think   AVERAGE MIND SET.

Blue-Green-Red People

I have been lecturing for years that there is NO SUCH THING AS BLACK OR WHITE PEOPLE.....OR BROWN PEOPLE...... OR YELLOW PEOPLE......

There are only Blue and Green and Red people. (Am I using a Label?) And folks turn around and look at me in a strange way and say to themselves..."this guy must be crazy...blue people?".

Yes....Blue People!

Blue People are Blue Chip people. People you can trust. People who are positive. People you like to be around. People you would want as a neighbor. People who are winners. People whom you would like your children to grow up and be like.

People who have that POSITIVE MIND SET. That's what BLUE people are.

RED people are the opposite of BLUE people. They create NEGATIVE FORCE. They are people you can not trust. People who point fingers and stab people in the back. Losers. Evil people. These RED people, you do not what to be around.

But…..most people fall into the third group…..GREEN PEOPLE.

It's like they are walking a fence. They can fall to the BLUE side or they can fall to the RED side…with just a little push they can go either way. Sometimes they are a Bluish Green or a Greenish Red.

The goal of any organization is to hire BLUE people who can lead GREEN people to make themselves better people and thus help the organization become more successful. The goal of any organization is to NOT hire any RED people because their negativity will destroy the organization.

Sooooooooo! There is no such thing as Black or White. In my way of thinking……SPECIAL MIND SET knows that people are Blue or Green or Red.

In Sports, many coaches who are AVERAGE MIND SET…. a 90%er…..want to WIN at any cost. They close their eyes and keep players on their team who are great athletes… BUT…..who are RED people. These coaches try to WIN with these RED people because WINNING at all costs is the only thing that counts in their mind.

As a Coach or as a person, I always wanted to find BLUE people. Or to help CREATE BLUE people.

In 47 years of coaching I never worried about WINNING. Yes….if you can believe it. This is a fact.

Why? Why do I feel this way?

I always believed and still do, that WINNING will take care of itself if we coach all the correct things…...on the field and off the field………during the season and in the off-season.

We would have to teach football skills BUT MORE importantly, we would have to teach human skills.

I knew that if we were POSITIVE MIND SET then we could be SPECIAL. SPECIAL MIND SET people are more coachable. They are more BLUE than anything else. And since PLAYERS WIN…...we as a team had a better chance for success.

The philosophy I used with my coaching staff was that we could have one or two RED players to start the season, with hopes and expectation that BLUE players would be able to influence those two RED players to make themselves better….help them move to the GREEN level.

Any more than two REDS on the team will produce disaster. Their NEGATIVE FORCE would beat us before we ever took a step on the field. They would demonstrate all the WEAKNESS of REDs……back stabbing….pointing finger at others for blame….Excusitis…..jealousy.

Results…..BAD TEAM MORALE…..DISASTER!

Some AVERAGE MIND SET coaches continue to accept RED players because they may be great athletes and the possibility of WINNING is the only thing that counts in their mind.

As mentioned. we could deal with two REDS at the start of the season but they had better get better and quick, as far as their attitude was. They had to become GREEN quickly or they were not long for our team.

Don't get me wrong. I want to WIN just like the other guy. To WIN we need players that can play the game to a high level of performance. We will give a chance to a RED but I have learned from experience that too many REDS,…no matter how good an athlete they are, will prove disastrous.

I always said to our team and coaching staff…..."WIN WHAT?"

"WIN a stink-in game so you sacrifice your standards?" "What message are we sending to the rest of the team when we try to WIN at all costs by lowering our standards." We send a message that we are NOT SPECIAL in a good way. We show that we are AVERAGE MIND SET…..ALL THE WAY!

In my way of thinking…a real LOSER!

If we are going to WIN…..let's WIN the correct way. Let's WIN with quality people….people who deserve to WIN. I do not want to WIN with BUMS!

The Weakness of Generalities-

Years ago I was teaching at an all-black school. One day I am in the teachers room and a white female teacher walks in and starts complaining about the students. She refers to the word "they". "They do this…they can't do that etc.,etc." I said….. "Hey….what about Kevin Bowie?" She said, "Oh, he is different". I said…"What about Sam Davis, Nokey Johnson, Sam Stepney etc.,etc." She continued to say…."Oh…they are different." I said…

"Yes…and don't forget it….they are different. Don't lump everyone together into a generality." The teacher was embarrassed and left the room.

In our society we have challenges with black and white differences. I say that most of the time it has nothing to do with color. It has to do with *class* of people or *type* of people. The proof is when people say as the teacher above stated….."Oh…he is different." Yes, people are all different and GENERALITIES are inaccurate and dangerous and characteristic of AVERAGE MIND SET…..

WEAKNESS…..NEGATIVE MIND SET! Eliminate this trait from your personality if it exists.

Sympathy

Many times during our life we will have opportunity to express *sympathy*.

When a friend experiences a death in their family, we show respect and our sensitivity to the situation by expressing our *sympathy*. This is a nice gesture on our part. But, as the years went by I started to question this expression of *sympathy*.

Let me give you a for instance…..an example.

A few years ago the wife of a very good friend of mine suddenly died of a brain aneurism. Naturally it was a tragedy for the entire family. The woman left a grieving husband and three children.

During the wake for my friend's wife, a few hundred people came to express their regrets.

A long line formed to go past her coffin and then to express their *sympathy* to the family.

One by one, the good people expressed their sorrow. Many were crying. I could see that my friend and his children were very distraught. They looked like they were feeling worse after all the people would express their own grief for the wife. When it came my turn to talk to my friend and his children, I said……"John…it's going to be all right. She has gone to a better place. You and the children are strong and she would

want you to carry on and have great lives." He said to me;…
…"thanks Theo…..I needed that."

What I tried to do was to give my friend and his children POSITIVE FORCE during a time when they were in great pain. Their friends expressed grief and sorrow and did not realize that they were giving NEGATIVE FORCE in the name of *sympathy*. These people thought they were doing right. After all, when someone dies, aren't you suppose to show sorrow? My friend John knew that I was trying to PUSH him up. He understood that I saw all the people try to be nice by expressing their grief and sorrow. We had talked many times in the past about POSITIVE and NEGATIVE FORCE and he understood what I did and why I said what I said. He was grateful and the POSITIVE words were just what he needed at that time.

I mention this example of NEGATIVE FORCE at this time in this book because in our normal everyday living …… sometimes we learn things or ways of behaving which can be *counter productive.*

Every person at that wake really wanted or hoped to say something to make John and the children feel better. But, what we think are the right words can get the wrong result. TERMINOLOGY AND PERCEPTION is so important. Sometimes we say things that do not help us accomplish our goal. Thus to be POSITIVE and SPECIAL MIND SET…. we have to do and say things that are POSITIVE AND SPECIAL.

We must learn to eliminate words of WEAKNESS.... NEGATIVITY from our daily speech.

Chapter 3
The Facts of Life

The FACTS OF LIFE are definitions of ideas I call concepts. Learning and using these concepts can help a person to become POSITIVE MIND SET…SPECIAL MIND SET.

Remember your goal. You want to become more POSITIVE and SPECIAL MIND SET.

These concepts are all common sense and NOT new. The only difference here is that you learn to NOT "keep these ideas in your back pocket"….instead…..learn these concepts and "use them daily." Keep them right in front of your nose ….on the front burner……so they are a constant reminder.

"We always want our own way"

From the time we are little children, we develop a behavior that… "we want our own way." When we are small and do not get our way….we cry to Mommy. Many times Mommy will give us our own way and we learn if we cry and complain then we can get our own way. Thus we have learned NEGATIVE behavior. This behavior carries over into our adult life and into our relationships with all kinds of people that we come into contact with. Everyone from loved ones…..people we work with……friends…relatives…..acquaintances etc.,.

If we are lucky, as we mature, we learn that we may still WANT OUR OWN WAY…..but sometimes it is better to NOT ALWAYS *GET* OUR OWN WAY. We learn that in relationships we can not always have our own way and sometimes it is better to NOT have our own way.

It is characteristic of STRENGTH……to not act like a baby and always insist on having our own way. We will talk more later about "give control to get control" and how this leads to POSITIVE MIND SET…SPECIAL MIND SET.

In our development of POSITIVE MIND SET…SPECIAL MIND SET,we have to learn to eliminate this NEGATIVE FORCE trait of "always wanting our own way." This is WEAKNESS.

"It's always about ourselves"-

Everything we do is always about ourselves.

Well, everyone knows this. Right?……

Maybe!

You talk with a Little League baseball coach and he says he loves working with young people so he can help them grow. He THINKS and SAYS he does it for THEM. ………………………..WRONG!

He does it for himself FIRST.

Yes, he does help the young men in his charge but he coaches Little League because it gives him great pleasure and satisfaction. It makes him feel like he is doing something good….something worthwhile. It makes him feel good about himself. It is FUN. FUN for him!

There is nothing WRONG with this. The coach SHOULD do things to make himself feel good. It improves his mental health. Better mental health makes for better physical health. This is good. The fact that he is helping others while he satisfies his emotional and psychological needs is great.But saying that he is doing it for the boys is not the WHOLE truth. Being SPECIAL MIND SET…the coach has to get under the water (remember the Iceberg Theory of Thinking)…. otherwise the coach is AVERAGE MIND SET.

The truth of the matter is that he is doing it for himself FIRST.

When we live in the SPECIAL MIND SET mode we are aware that "it is always about ourselves." Everything we do is ALWAYS ABOUT OURSELVES….FIRST!

AVERAGE MIND SET people will give you an argument on this concept. But, I believe that if they "go under the water" they will understand that this concept is TRUE.

"We are a Total of our Life Experiences"-

Yes….we are a total of our life experiences.

The Good…the Bad and the Ugly.

From the day we are born our life experiences help to make us what we are.

Good parents try to protect their children by putting them in environments that may help their children to grow up and develop into better people. You do not need an engineering degree to know this simple fact. Parents try to move to better neighborhoods. Parents work themselves to the bone to send their kids to better schools. In trying to understand people…. or ourselves, we must understand this concept.

In doing so, we have a better chance of understanding the people we are communicating with. We can better understand why people are NEGATIVE or why they may be POSITIVE. We can better understand how people learn to be SPECIAL MIND SET as compared to AVERAGE MIND SET.

In teaching and coaching, I would try to sell my assistant coaches that when dealing with a 16 or 17 year old person, remember it took that person 16-17 years to get the way they are.

We are not going to change that person in 6 days or 6 weeks. This is not to say that we will not try to communicate with that person and hope for some behavior modification. We do not know what level of development that person has reached as far as their MIND SET is concerned. Thus we TRY to communicate with that person by SELLING our ideas.

This is true leadership.

Just telling someone to do something is not good enough. We are not working with robots. We are working with people who are very complex. This is where TRUST comes into play.More about TRUST and SELLING is discussed later on in this book.

Excusitis-Dr. Kern Thompson

Excusitis! A disease we acquire from birth.

We learn as small children that if we can make a GOOD excuse….an excuse that sounds like it is true…..our mother will not holler at us.

An example; I drop a glass of milk. The glass falls to the floor and breaks. What a mess! The first thing I do is tell my mother that it wasn't my fault. The glass was wet and slippery. It wasn't my fault. I try to make an excuse. My mother calms down and doesn't get too angry. Wow! I got over on that one!

This is a simple example but I am sure you get the message. We learn when we are very young to make excuses. *As we get older we still make excuses.* We say things like…. "it wasn't my fault"…..or we POINT FINGERS at someone else and say it was their fault.

In developing SPECIAL MIND SET we have to eliminate the disease of EXCUSITIS.

As a coach, I had players who would try to make excuses for a bad play. I would try and sell my players of a better behavior.

Eliminate the excuses.

It doesn't matter. The bad play occurred and we have NO CONTROL over it NOW....after it happened....get over it....move on. It is over. Yesterday's news. Move on. Don't spend valuable time worrying about the bad play *otherwise it may affect our future performance in a negative way.* Spending time on EXCUSITIS will take away from our FOCUS on the next play.

This type of MIND SET is POSITIVE thinking. SPECIAL thinking.

I learned from the great football coach Vince Lombardi of the Green Bay Packers who said......RECOVER instantaneously......don't waste time and energy on yesterday's news. This was SPECIAL MIND SET. The MIND SET of WINNERS.

I learned as a coach that I did not want to hear EXCUSES. If a player was late for practice. I did not want to hear why? If I listened to an EXCUSE, then I would have to make a judgment.... "is he telling me the truth?" Since I do not have mental telepathy, I can not determine a truth from a falsehood. Thus, I trained my players to never give me an excuse. The Goal here was to eliminate THE DISEASE…. EXCUSITIS!

The player would learn to move from the AVERAGE MIND SET mode of using EXCUSITIS to the SPECIAL MIND SET mode by using SPECIAL behavior of NOT using an excuse.

"Give Control to get control"

So often we want our own way. This is understandable.

We always want our own way as was stated previously. But, when we learn to give others *their* way, we will find out that many times we get our own way……..anyway!

An example;

A husband and wife are going to go out on a Saturday night to the movies. The husband says to the wife…."Let's go see ….(a specific movie title)." The husband does not ask the wife what movie she wants to see….he simply makes a suggestion based on his desire to see a specific movie.

My suggestion is that the husband should have asked his wife….. "What movie do you want to see?"….or he may give his wife several choices of movies playing in the local theatre. In this way, *he gave his wife control.* Is she happy? Yes…… what a nice guy. He asked his wife what she wanted to see.

Chances are the movie she selects may be a movie he would also like to see.

The wife may even say….. "Gee, I don't know….what would you like to see?" She puts the choice right back into his lap. Now he can select the movie of his choice. Seeing the movie of his choice is really no big deal. He had a chance to make his wife happy by giving her control of the decision. In return, he ended up with the control. Give control to get control.

The Cynic may say that this type of behavior is "being tricky"….to get your own way. The truth of the matter is…. it is a lot more pleasurable making other people happy than being selfish and always trying to have your own way.

When a person grows up and learns this fact, they mature to the point where they are no longer living in a AVERAGE MIND SET mode. They are living in a SPECIAL MIND SET mode.

It doesn't always work out like the example I mentioned above but many times it does and you are better for it. Strength shows that you do not have to ALWAYS HAVE YOUR OWN WAY. And……at the same time you can make other people HAPPY….and feel good.

In return, they like you better. Doing this is a WIN, WIN SITUATION. As I mentioned before, the Cynic will say that this is manipulation. I say….remember….*What is your Goal?*

The Goal is better communication....better relationship....better feeling between two people....better everything.

Take a negative and turn it into a positive-

This is a great SKILL that we must learn. Normal, everyday people, can learn from athletes and coaches who have taken failure and *turned the failure into a positive by learning from the failure.*

We say that PAIN is good if we learn from the PAIN. (The olde expression….NO PAIN, NO GAIN) If we do not learn from the PAIN (failure), then the experience was for nothing.

AVERAGE MIND SET will not learn from the NEGATIVE….the PAIN.

They will make excuses for the failure. It wasn't their fault. They will point fingers to others for the failure. These are all traits and characteristics of a loser.

I am sorry to say….they are characteristics of AVERAGE MIND SET.

POSITIVE MIND SET…SPECIAL MIND SET….look at failure as an opportunity to learn. WOW! I guess this sounds high fa-lutin!!!! Do you like that word?

Well, to be SPECIAL MIND SET…..you have to do SPECIAL things….NOT AVERAGE things.

It is SPECIAL MIND SET to ALWAYS take a NEGATIVE and turn it into a POSITIVE. This is NOT AVERAGE thinking.

Winners always learn from their failures.
You can do it! No excuses.

Chapter 4
Communication...The Big C

The number ONE system a person has to develop in the development of People Skills is *Communication*.

Poor communication will lead to "problems" faster than anything else. If we are to get better in all relationships.... at home.....at work.....socially.....etc., we MUST MASTER our Communication skills.

If we are a teacher...a coach....a supervisor...a business owner....a Company CEO....a leader of any type or a person who has hopes of living a better life.....PEOPLE SKILLS and the ART OF COMMUNICATION must be learned.

Our skills must be worked on daily.

This number ONE system, Communication, can help guarantee us the chance to be POSITIVE MIND SET... SPECIAL MIND SET and on the road to better mental health which leads to better physical health. And guess what else? ....

HAPPINESS!

Dr. Janice Glaser and Dr. Ronald Glaser have done a number of studies of the affect of mental health on physical health. They are worth reading and their books can be found in any library or good Book Store.

Please consider the following as Concepts of Communication which must be mastered to be POSITIVE MIND SET….. SPECIAL MIND SET….

Terminology and Perception.

Terminology is the words we use to communicate. Perception is the understanding by other people of the words we use. Wow…..is this important!

How often have we said to other people….."I didn't say that."…..or "I didn't mean that." I wish I had a dollar for every time that has happened to me. I could compete for Bill Gates and his money. Just joking…of course.

So often we speak to people and ASSUME…they heard us….or they understood us…..just because we were talking to them. It doesn't always happen. Sometimes, what we say goes over their head or in one ear and out the other.

I picked up a word some time ago from a friend, Ron Feldhun, one of my assistant coaches. The word is "clutter". "Clutter" meaning that we have all kinds of thoughts going through our head all day long. Sometimes when we talk with someone our mind is elsewhere and we really do not get the message that our friend who is talking to us is trying to convey. This "clutter" affects our PERCEPTION.

Another word I believe to be very important is "Timing". We hear this word used in many different situations. We say….."to be in the right place at the right time." Aw….."timing". Thus in communication….. "timing" is important because we can say something today and the person we are talking to doesn't hear us…..but several days later we say the same thing and our friend HEARS US. "Timing" and "Clutter"…..have a lot to do with Communication. So, do not get upset if the person we are talking to doesn't HEAR us. Understanding these concepts…..*Timing* and *Clutter*…… will help us develop a POSITIVE MIND SET….which in reality is also a SPECIAL MIND SET……and don't forget the 90-10 rule!

Fair-

Probably one of the words we should eliminate from our vocabulary is FAIR. The longer you live the more you understand that many times life is NOT FAIR.

It is a nice thought to think that we are being treated FAIRLY or we treat others in a FAIR manner. But….. again….remember…. FAIR is always the other person's PERCEPTION. Perception is reality to a person we are communicating with….but……their perception may be wrong…. thus what they think is *reality* is NOT!

Working as a teacher and coach for 47 years, on occasion I would have a player say that one of my assistant coaches was NOT FAIR.

"Coach Brown is not fair!"……..."Coach Johnson is not fair!"……I knew these men to be very fair people but I knew the only thing that counted was the perception of the player.

The Mind Set of the player thinking my assistant coach was NOT FAIR would affect the performance of the player and thus affect the team in a NEGATIVE way. Thus, I tried to teach my staff a concept;

"It is NOT only important to be fair….but it is MORE important to APPEAR TO BE FAIR."

Thus, when a situation came up as I just described, my assistant coach was instructed to FIX this situation as soon as possible by having a one on one meeting with the player and try to INCREASE POSITIVE COMMUNICATION. Try to find out Why? And How? The person misunderstood the attempt at communication. To FIX the misperception is very important if we are to increase productivity.

Remember……to be SPECIAL we must do SPECIAL THINGS!

Two ears and one mouth- philosopher Epictetus

God gave us two ears and one mouth. Maybe we should listen twice as much as we speak.

For a teacher or coach this is hard because we are always lecturing or instructing….we are always talking.

In Communication it can be helpful if we ask the other person a question and then shut our mouth and listen. *Two ears and one mouth.* The comments made by the person we are talking to will tell us what question to ask next or the comments by that person will give us important information which can make for better communication and or instruction.

The comments will also tell us the person's MIND SET….. or his perception of a situation……or at the very least….our perception of his perception.

In communication I am always trying to get INTERACTION between myself and the person I am talking with. Learn to listen more than we speak. This is SPECIAL behavior.

The next time you go to a party or a picnic, just listen to other people talk and talk and talk. *They really are not interested* in what you have to say. They really are *only interested* in what they are saying. Did you ever notice that? It is funny. Try it…the next party you go to. You will have some laughs.

Very seldom will a person ask you a question. When this happens, they are interested in your answer otherwise they probably would not ask you a question.

Other people will just talk and talk and even try to talk louder than you…talk over you….so they can be heard. They really are MORE interested in what they have to say than what you have to say! AVERAGE OR SPECIAL MIND SET?????????? You answer the question.

It Must be for a Reason-

This is a phrase I use all the time. It helps SELL an idea. By stressing *It Must Be for a Reason,* it sells the idea WHY we are doing what we do. If you can sell WHY (the Reason)…… you have a better chance of selling an idea. A better chance at COMMUNICATION. Everything is for a reason. Sooooooo explain the reason.

This is a very important concept and very often in my communication with someone, I will say to myself….or to the person I am talking with….. "What is the reason….. why is this person saying this……IT MUST BE FOR A REASON".

If possible, I must make sure that I know the REASON otherwise if I guess the REASON, I could guess wrong and my PERCEPTION, my understanding of what the person is trying to say….is all wrong. Thus, I get the wrong message. Result……..NEGATIVE problems!

Don't be afraid or embarrassed to ask questions. Eliminate embarrassment from your personality. WOW! You say this is a hard thing to do. Yes it is! But embarrassment is a wasted emotion and usually counter productive. Embarrassment can stop you from doing or saying what you should, thus stopping you from reaching your goal. Embarrassment in this case is a sign of WEAKNESS…..something that is done when we are in the AVERAGE MIND SET MODE.

Sell….don't tell-

This is a tough one. *Sell…..don't tell.*

So often when we talk to people, we talk and talk and talk. What we are really doing is telling…telling….telling.

What is our *Goal* when we talk to these people? Are we trying to convince them on an idea? Are we trying to SELL them? If we are trying to sell an idea…..telling will not get it done! We have to sell our idea. Selling occurs when you get *interaction* with the person you are communicating with. Instead of *telling*….ask the person a question that you already know the answer to. Using the logic mentioned above….*It Must be for a Reason*

Try this example; I am talking with one of my players about how much time he should spend in the weight room in the off-season. I could *tell* him that he should be in the weight room four days a week. Instead, I ask the player a question….."How many days a week should you be in the weight room and tell me WHY?"

Hopefully the player will say four days a week and he will tell me WHY by saying that the more time invested in the weight room, the bigger, faster and stronger he will become.

By using this technique of SELLING……you did not TELL the player. Instead, *it came from him.* He actually TOLD you what he should do. You as a coach did not TELL him what he should do. He said it…it came from his lips.

If the person gives you the answer you expected. Great. You created interaction. You sold the idea. Or, the person sold himself. Asking WHY?... Gives you the feedback you need to know. If the person gives an unacceptable answer….give more information about your idea and continue to ask the question……TELL ME WHY? Hopefully this time the answer will be to your liking. Hopefully the person will be on the same page with you. This is communication at it's best.

DO NOT LECTURE PEOPLE. Give them a chance to speak back to you. You can SELL your ideas by using this technique or the person you are talking to, may SELL you on their idea. This is good. You have an open mind. You have interaction back and forth. SPECIAL MIND SET…. NOT…..AVERAGE MIND SET.

Let me break this concept down even better.

If I believe in an idea, it belongs to me. I own it. If I lecture to you about my idea and get no feedback from you, I have NO idea if you understand me or believe me or BUY my idea.

That makes sense, doesn't it?

If I SELL you on my idea, you bought it and now you OWN it. It belongs to you. Thus, I have to ask you a question to create feedback. Your answer (Remember Two ears and One Mouth) will tell me if you have accepted the idea or not. Accepting the idea will tell me you BOUGHT it. If your answer to my question tells me that you do *not* accept my idea, then I now must add more information about my idea and then ask another question. The process may sound complicated but it really isn't.

Simply stated......give information and then ask a question. Keep giving information until you made yourself clear and continue asking questions until you and the person you are talking to are on the same page.

Finally, you have reached a point where you have sold your idea to the other person. Only by using interaction and feedback can you FIND out if the person you are talking to, BOUGHT your idea. SELL.......DON'T TELL. Makes for better communication.

When we are in the AVERAGE MIND SET mode, we lecture to people. When we are in the SPECIAL MIND SET mode, we SELL people on our ideas by using SELLING techniques, not TELLING techniques.

If we are in a leadership position, What is our Goal? If we are to LEAD and get people to do what they should do.....

productivity is higher when people believe in what we say and suggest. SELL….DON'T TELL!

The cynic will say that the person may just tell you what you want to hear. That is possible…but remember……it came from his lips and if that person doesn't do what he said he should do, you can always come back to him and remind him that he is hurting his credibility. Please believe me when I say that this system really works.

Because of the many accomplishments that I have been blessed to achieve, people have called me a great motivator. I have always stressed that I do not want to considered a great motivator……instead I like to think that in order to be a great motivator, one needs to be a GREAT COMMUNICATOR.

Hard or Soft-

Many times I have had people I work with, say to me…. "Coach, you are hard". I would always respond…… *"I do not want to be hard….I want to be right."* So often when we are trying to be what we think is right ……..it appears we are being hard.

A parent wants their teenage son to come home before midnight on a Saturday night. The son feels his parents are being too hard. After all, his friends are allowed to stay out longer on Saturday nights. In this case the parents are *not trying to be hard,* they are trying (in their mind) *to be right.*

They believe that 12 midnight is late enough for their teenage son to be out on a Saturday night.

I as a teacher and coach always tried to hold my students or players accountable for their actions. If they were late for a meeting, they would have to make up for the lateness with an assignment of some sort. Many times I was considered as being HARD. I would try to *sell* the student or player that I was trying to be RIGHT and not hard. I was trying to maintain my credibility. I was trying to make sure that the student or player was being held accountable for their actions. I was trying to sell them on a leadership technique that they could adopt later in life when they were in a leadership role.

Push people up –

In communication, POSITIVE MIND SET people will always try to PUSH PEOPLE UP….NOT DOWN. Pushing People Up is also a trait of SPECIAL MIND SET.

When a person is weak, they need to push folks down and put themselves above others. This is what happens so often when we consider racial prejudice. Thus, PUSHING PEOPLE DOWN is NEGATIVE FORCE…. NEGATIVE MIND SET….AVERAGE MIND SET…all the way.

People will like to be around you if you are the type of person who PUSHES PEOPLE UP.

Your personal relationships at home or at work or in any social setting have a better chance to be successful if you can master this important concept of Communication.

Hate-

What a terrible word in the English language.

It is also a word that is probably misused more often than not. People say "I hate that"...or "I hate him". Hate is a very strong word. It is a powerful NEGATIVE FORCE word. Try to use other words in your daily communication. Hate is a subjective word....an emotional word. Remember, *it is difficult to make objective decisions when we are emotional*. It is almost impossible. Try to eliminate this word from your dictionary. Don't use NEGATIVE FORCE.

When I hear the word HATE, I know that the person I am talking with is in the NEGATIVE MIND SET...AVERAGE MIND SET mode.

I have heard people, in casual conversation, say that they "hate" a certain person. How can you "hate" someone? "Hate" is TOO powerful a word to be used in this example of casual conversation. The person could use other words.... such as "I don't respect that person"...or whatever....but to say "Hate".......Naw...this is AVERAGE MIND SET vocabulary

Defuse-

Defuse is a great communication technique to use. In communication, so often the conversation comes to a point where it becomes what can be called an argument. One person wants to win the argument over the other person. Remember the concept…. "We always want our own way." The combatants start to become loud and hostile. The only thing here that can happen is POOR COMMUNICATION. One person will NOT SELL THE OTHER…that is for sure.

Remember….*everyone wants their own way* and that's for sure in an argument. DEFUSE. Take away the other person's weapons. In an argument, the combatants raise their gloves like they were in a boxing ring. DEFUSE. Get the combatant to drop his gloves. You may need to use the technique of….. *"give control to get control."*

A POSITIVE MIND SET person is SPECIAL MIND SET and can give up control. Weakness or AVERAGE MIND SET can never give up control and thus never learns to DEFUSE.

DEFUSE is a communication concept…..a technique that must be mastered in order to reach POSITIVE MIND SET…..SPECIAL MIND SET….and be in the 10% mode. Learning to DEFUSE can help in the development of your technique of *sell…not tell.*

To Defuse is to BACK OFF……don't throw wood on the fire….don't make it worse by what words you use…..don't get caught up in trying to win the conversation. It isn't really that important…is it?   Show strength….

NEGATIVE-AVERAGE MIND SET would think that they would have to WIN the argument at all costs.

POSITIVE-SPECIAL MIND SET has THICK SKIN and is not bothered by losing a conversation. So What! Big Deal!

You must remember one of your major goals. *The goal of being more successful at whatever you do.* These people skills of communication MUST be mastered if you are to reach your GOAL of greater success.

Get excited….. enthusiasm is caught, not taught!

In communication….either through the use of words when we speak….or though the use of BODY LANGUAGE…. it is a characteristic of POSITIVE MIND SET people and SPECIAL MIND SET people that they demonstrate excitement and enthusiasm.

Do you like to be around dull people? Does it motivate you up to be around deadhead people?

Some people are alive but they are DEAD in spirit.

POSITIVE people are fun to be around. They are SPECIAL. WOW!... "I like that person."

In the work place, people have said…. "boy…it is no fun around here."

In teaching, I have heard teachers complain about the atmosphere….the attitude amongst the teachers and administrators in the school.

Who is responsible? Should we blame others or should we take the Bull by the Horns and do something about it? You answer the question. Put yourself and fire and walk around with enthusiasm. Radiate with excitement….humor….and enthusiasm.

What is AVERAGE MIND SET in this scenario and what is SPECIAL MIND SET?

What is NEGATIVE MIND SET and what is POSITIVE MIND SET in this situation?

SPECIAL MIND SET….POSITIVE MIND SET people step up and *do something about the situation.* They do not wait for things to change by themselves.

Let me tell you a great story I heard back in 1961. The story teller was Paul "Bear" Bryant, the legendary football coach from the University of Alabama. Coach Bryant was trying to explain how ENTHUSIASM IS CAUGHT….NOT TAUGHT;

I am paraphrasing but the story goes like this;

"A man gets a can of gasoline. He goes out of his house and stands in the street and pours the can of gasoline all over himself. He takes a match and puts himself on fire. What happens? All the neighbors come out of their houses. Cars stop in the road. People are screaming….yelling….."that man is on fire"….. "that man is on fire." Yes……. *"that man is on fire.""* Put yourself on FIRE and people will come and watch you. "Get excited…..Fire in the belly…..Enthusiasm is caught not taught!"

It's just a story….but I liked it and I have told this story many times over the years. The key point is that….you…. yes you….have to get excited. You have to put yourself on FIRE. You have to have FIRE IN THE BELLY! SPECIAL MIND SET PEOPLE DO THIS. POSITIVE MIND SET PEOPLE DO THIS.

Dull…..average mind set…..negative mind set people just complain and continue to make excuses…..point fingers… give off negative vibes etc.,etc.,.

COMMUNICATION …..people skills…..must be mastered in order to move from the NEGATIVE MIND SET… AVERAGE MIND SET stage to the POSITIVE MIND SET…SPECIAL MIND SET mode.

Sell a Dream-

Learn to SELL A DREAM.

This is a great skill…..a great technique that must be learned by the person who hopes to be a POSITIVE MIND SET…SPECIAL MIND SET person. This ability to PUSH PEOPLE UP and SELL A DREAM….instead of taking a dream away from someone…..is key to the development of POSITIVE and…SPECIAL MIND SET.

If you are in a position of leadership of any kind…..in any organization. You MUST learn to SELL DREAMS. Let me repeat this concept. You MUST learn to SELL DREAMS. You MUST BE A DREAM MAKER!!!!!! Only by selling a dream will people follow you.

Sell a dream is a people skill that can be used by people in a leadership role in business or any work place or by a friend or a relative. By selling people on the great possibilities of what they CAN do will endear these people to you.

By PUSHING UP people they will want to be around you. You make them feel good. You make them feel worthy. They will TRUST you to a higher level. They will take suggestion from you. They will be loyal to you. In short, they will bust their tail for you.

This is what will happen in MOST cases. Of course, if you are dealing with a NEGATIVE person, the person may not respond in positive fashion.

Selling a dream and pushing people up **should NOT be about what it can do for you.** Those good things that come back to you, come back because of your POSITIVE behavior and are some of the rewards of doing what is right. The reason you try to sell a dream to people is because it is the *right* *thing to do.* This type of behavior on your part demonstrates POSITIVE MIND SET...SPECIAL MIND SET.

John Wooten, the legendary basketball coach of UCLA said a great statement; "You can NOT have a perfect day unless you do something for someone and that person can never repay you for that something."

In other words…..Do it because it is the RIGHT thing to do!

When we are in a leadership role, we are trying to lead our group, our team, our organization to MAXIMUM PRODUCTIVITY. Selling DREAMS and PUSHING UP people puts you in the eyes of other people as being very, VERY SPECIAL. These same people will respond to your leadership because you are POSITIVE about them and you are POSITIVE about your ideas. It becomes easier to SELL them on your ideas. They will give a greater commitment because of their increased TRUST in you. They like being around you. They will follow you.

As a teacher and coach, I took over losing football programs and the GOAL was to "bring them back from the dead" as one newspaper said. In order to create the MIND SET necessary, I had to SELL DREAMS. Part of the fun of living……part of the fun of communication is being a DREAM MAKER!!!!!!

Chapter 5
Don't Worry About the Things We Have No Control Over-

This was a concept I had to sell and teach to my football players for all of the 47 years I was a football coach.

As an insurance and securities salesman for two years, I had to sell this concept to my team of salespeople.

People......worry and worry and worry so much about things THEY HAVE NO CONTROL OVER. Thus I developed the following concept in my teaching;

Two Types of Life Experiences-

Basically, there are two types of Life Experiences.

One type of experiences are those we HAVE CONTROL OF. The second type of experiences are those WE HAVE *NO* CONTROL OF.

AVERAGE MIND SET people worry about things they have no control over. Athletes and coaches worry about the weather….the officials. We have no control of the weather or what officials do in a game. People make themselves sick over worry of things they have NO CONTROL OF.

To worry about things we have NO control over takes away our real focus on the challenge at hand.

I have seen it over and over again in sports where the coach wastes time and energy trying to get in the ear of the officials. I did this myself as a young coach. Then I got smarter and realized that it did no good. I omitted the officials from the game because I had NO control over them. What a positive difference.

My productivity increased because I didn't waste time on something I had NO control of. Instead I spent my time in areas that I DID have control and my team's results became more successful. FINALLY, I started to learn how to be SPECIAL MIND SET.

It is a waste of precious energy. It is a waste of time. NEGATIVE force is controlling people who worry about things they have NO CONTROL OF.

This worry of things we have NO control over is characteristic of being in the AVERAGE MIND SET…NOT SPECIAL MIND SET mode. Remember the 90-10 rule.

POSITIVE MIND SET people……SPECIAL MIND SET people…..have trained themselves to worry only about the things they DO HAVE CONTROL OF. Now....they can do something about these things. Now they are putting their time towards something that CAN be altered or affected.

It is important that we constantly remind ourselves….. "is this something I can control????? Or am I wasting my time….I have no control." This is an important technique in training oneself to be SPECIAL MIND SET…..POSITIVE MIND SET……..a 10% person….Not a 90% person. Remember the 90-10 rule?????

When I learned this technique…this concept…..my health improved tremendously. My blood pressure problems went away. My MIND SET got better…….MY MIND SET got healthier and consequently my physical health got better.

Chapter 6
Don't Allow the Elements To Affect Your Performance in A Negative Way-

From the time we are children, we learn to allow things to bother us. We grow up being what I call AVERAGE MIND SET. If we are lucky we learn to be better. I call this SPECIAL MIND SET. In AVERAGE MIND SET….we allow *negative force elements* to affect us in *a negative way*.

When we have unsuccessful experiences or when anything negative happens, we are affected in a negative way. We are sad. We are disappointed. Physically we are stressed and feel poorly. We can actually get sick. Thus I use the concept…… Thick Skin as compared to Thin Skin.

Thick Skin or Thin Skin-

This is not new. Everyone has heard of this saying before. But, I suggest in order for us to develop a POSITIVE MIND SET and become SPECIAL MIND SET, we need to constantly remind ourselves…… "what are we going to do?" Be… Thick Skin or be Thin Skin? Be weak or be strong? Be AVERAGE MIND SET or be SPECIAL MIND SET? Stay POSITIVE or allow NEGATIVITY to affect us in a NEGATIVE way. It is our DECISION. We HAVE CONTROL. WE HAVE CONTROL! WE HAVE CONTROL!

If we train ourselves to be Thick Skinned…..we can USE *negative force* to motivate us to overcome a challenge. We must learn to RECOVER instantaneously…..and attack our challenge (problem) and make ourselves stronger. We must learn to attack challenges (problems) and not run away from these challenges. Did you ever notice that when we try to avoid a "problem," the "problem" doesn't go away. Tomorrow, the "problem" is still there. SPECIAL MIND SET learns this lesson and attacks the problem as soon as possible. SPECIAL MIND SET doesn't procrastinate.

We have a poem in our Football Bible which deserves repeating at this time.

On the Plains of Hesitation

On the Plains of Hesitation lie the bleached bones of countless millions.

Who, when on the threshold of success,

Decided to rest….

And while resting…..

On the Plains of Hesitation….

THEY DIED

-George W. Cecil

We have CONTROL. We have CONTROL how we react and handle these negative force experiences. No excuses. We have CONTROL. This is an important step in developing POSITIVE MIND SET and becoming SPECIAL MIND SET.

We MUST use the *negative force to motivate us, not to discourage us.*

THICK SKIN allows us to OVERCOME and continue towards our goal.

THIN SKIN makes us weak and looking for excuses (EXCUSITIS) to NOT continue towards our goal.

Everyone Takes It Personal-

This is a phrase I use to further describe AVERAGE MIND SET behavior. Everyone takes it personal. Well, not everyone! SPECIAL MIND SET people have trained themselves to NOT BE…..*EVERYONE!* If we consider EVERYONE to be average……90%'ers……then we do NOT want to be in that category.

DON'T TAKE IT PERSONAL.

Let a negative force experience be like "rain falling off your shoulder." It means nothing. Tomorrow, *one billion plus Chinese people will not even k*now *that it happened.*

So often I sell people who are stressed out over a negative force experience…. "What does it mean?" "A year from today…. will you remember what happened today?" In most cases the person will NEVER remember what happened today a year from now…..or even a month or week from now and ……………

THEY ALLOW THE ELEMENTS TO AFFECT THEIR PERFORMANCE IN A NEGATIVE WAY.

Criticism is GOOD-

Criticism is GOOD? What do you mean? When we are in the AVERAGE MIND SET mode, we have learned to NOT want to hear criticism. It makes us feel bad. And…we do not want to feel bad. Do you want to feel bad?

Be POSITIVE when you hear criticism. Consider it, the criticism, an OPPORTUNITY to learn.

As a football coach for 47 years and teacher for 31 years, I always tried to sell my players and students that it was important for me to use objective criticism towards them. Only by receiving this evaluation can they help themselves become better.

I was trying to train my players and students to be SPECIAL MIND SET.

I used a saying….. "if the coach doesn't shout at you….. chances are he doesn't even know you are around."

In coaching, on many teams, the first string players usually get most of the criticism…..most of the coaching. Second and third string players unfortunately do NOT get most of the criticism or coaching. They, the second and third stringers actually should get more criticism and coaching so they can develop quicker and be in position to challenge the first stringers. The SPECIAL MIND SET coach understands this very important concept.

Everyone has to learn to be THICK SKINNED…… DON'T TAKE IT PERSONAL (in a negative way)…..learn to not be a 90%er……move from AVERAGE MIND SET to SPECIAL MIND SET……and stay POSITIVE MIND SET.

Chapter 7
Challenges and Solutions-

How many times have you heard a person say…"I've got problems….I've got problems."

WOW!

Like no one else in the world has problems.

One of the fun things about living is we learn to become *problem solvers*. This is fun!

Fun …you say. Is this guy crazy?

SPECIAL MIND SET….POSITIVE MIND SET says YES it is fun!

In life we learn that once we get rid of one "problem"….. another "problem" pops up. Since I was in college I started to use a THINGS TO DO list. As I got rid of one THING another THING popped up and I had to add this new

THING to my list. The list never ends. So What? Get used to it. Enjoy the daily challenge of being a *problem solver*.

The word PROBLEM is a NEGATIVE word. Thus I changed the word PROBLEM to the word CHALLENGE. CHALLENGE is a positive word. WOW! Another example of POSITIVE MIND SET. Thus we have CHALLENGES and SOLUTIONS.

Working with people who would say they have a PROBLEM, I would ask, "*and what is your solution…..what is your plan to get rid of the problem?*"
More often than not, the person would say they haven't come up with a solution yet. Or, they do not have a plan to solve the problem. In a nice way I would *try to sell* them on getting off the crying mode of complaining about their problems and do something about them. Thus move from NEGATIVE MIND SET…AVERAGE MIND SET…to POSITIVE MIND SET…SPECIAL MIND SET.

I would try to sell the idea that they need to come up with a solution. If it works…great. If the solution doesn't work… great also! What? How can that also be great? We know it is not great but instead of getting down and feeling sorry for yourself, just come up with another solution until you have mastered the "problem." THIS IS POSITIVE MIND SET. This is ***certainly*** an example of SPECIAL MIND SET not AVERAGE MIND SET, where the person would get depressed and upset that the solution didn't work out and just quit trying or worse, get into a NEGATIVE emotional state and get sick.

This is training of the mind.

We are a total of our life experiences and when we start out in life, we somehow learned to get upset and depressed if we try to fix a "problem" and it doesn't work out in a positive fashion. Thus we have to train ourselves to be POSITIVE MIND SET....SPECIAL MIND SET.

Remember the 90-10 rule. We want to be a 10 percenter.... SPECIAL MIND SET......not a 90 percenter which is... AVERAGE MIND SET.

A CHALLENGE is like climbing a mountain. Once we start climbing the mountain we hit all kinds of problems. We have to climb through trees and bushes....over holes....sand....all kinds of distractions to discourage us from continuing the climb up the mountain. It is the same when we climb the Mountain of Life Experiences.

Some people decide to stop after a few hard steps up the mountain. Others decide to stop in the middle of the climb up the mountain. Others decide to struggle and continue until they reach the top of the mountain.

Who is demonstrating AVERAGE OR SPECIAL MIND SET? Time to remember the poem... "On the Plains of Hesitation"

Sometimes, when we get to the top of the mountain we find out that.... "holly cow.....there is another mountain to climb on the other side". Now we have to make a decision. Continue or stop. No problem. Whatever you decide is

OK. But remember, it is your decision. Only the SPECIAL MIND SET will continue. It is your decision.

Thomas Edison had over 10,000 failures in his experiments before he discovered the filament for the electric light bulb. I dare say he was a great example of VERY SPECIAL MIND SET…..POSITIVE MIND SET. In fact Edison was credited with saying, " I do not mind failure because with each failure I know I am getting closer to success."

WOW!

SPECIAL….POSITIVE MIND SET ALL THE WAY! He was a man who overcame the *fear of failure* and he didn't use *excusitis* to stop him. SPECIAL MIND SET BABY…. SPECIAL ALL THE WAY.

Mistakes and decisions-

Many times when I talk to a group…..an organization of some type. I get a little cute and say, "you have never committed a mistake." This usually gets a few raised eyebrows. Of course we have all made mistakes. We make mistakes everyday and as long as we live we are going to make mistakes.

Let me explain why I use this technique….this statement. When we make a decision it is usually based on all the information we have at hand and our goal is to make a successful decision. We do not say…. "Gee….I hope this decision will fail." We hope to make a successful decision.

What really happens is we make a decision and if it works out, people say, "What a great decision!" If the decision doesn't work out, people say, "You made a mistake." I say….. nonsense.

We made a good decision…..based on all the information at hand and if it works out to the good….fine. If the decision doesn't work out…...it was a good decision but the decision just didn't work out.

Usually *timing* has a lot to do with whether or not the decision ends up a success or failure. We could make a decision today and it works. Tomorrow we could make the same decision and it doesn't work out satisfactory. We get all caught up in *mistakes*. The *mistake* is not important. *How we handle the mistake is what is most important.*

Do we learn from the mistake? Do we take this negative and turn it into a positive? Or, do we beat ourselves up because we made a so called *mistake.* People in SPECIAL MIND SET treat mistakes differently than people who are in a AVERAGE MIND SET mode.

SPECIAL MIND SET people take a so called mistake and come up with another solution. In fact, these people learn from the failure of the decision.

AVERAGE MIND SET "take it personal" when a so called mistake occurs.

They get depressed. More often than not, they discontinue the effort and do no come up with another solution. They use EXCUSITIS and run away from the CHALLENGE.

It is your decision. Don't lie to yourself. Understand you are either or. *You are* NEGATIVE MIND SET…AVERAGE MIND SET……*or You are* POSITIVE MIND SET…. SPECIAL MIND SET.

It is your DECISION!

Chapter 8
God and the Devil

What is this????? A book on religion???

NO……………..But I do believe in God. I know all about the BIG BANG theory. I believe in the BIG BANG, The only difference is that I believe GOD created the BIG BANG. When I think of God…..I think that God is the King of all the POSITIVE. Then I say to myself….if that is true…. and I believe that it is TRUE….then who is the King of all NEGATIVE? The answer has to be the Devil.

Oooh….the Devil.

Some people do not like to talk about the Devil. In fact sometimes when I talk about the Devil….people say…. "Is this a cult???" I laugh like heck. No….this is not a cult! This is about God being the King of all POSITIVE and the Devil the King of all NEGATIVE…simple as that.

I worked one year with Native Americans…..American Indians. They believe in evil spirits and understand the Devil concept.

I have worked with and lived with Black Americans and they too will talk about the Devil.

But, my own people…..white folk……they don't like to talk about the Devil.

White people blame everything on God. If something good happens they say…God did it. If something bad happens…. they say …."God had a reason for it to happen." Nonsense. If a man rapes three women and kills all three of them….are you telling me that God had a good reason for this to happen? I don't think so. I think that the evil one…the Devil did the deed by using man to do his dirty work. Now….this is my belief and I know you may or may not agree. OK….it is your choice. I have no problem with that. But….this is what I believe.

God is the King of POSITIVE FORCE. The Devil is the KING of NEGATIVE FORCE.

Back in 1985 I was teaching at Rahway High School in Rahway, New Jersey. The Principal of the school asked me to be present while he did a body search of a student who was suspected of carrying drugs. The boy was a 9th grade student whom I knew. He was carrying $600 in cash and wearing a long fur coat that cost a pretty penny. The Principal confiscated a quantity of drugs on the young man and the police had to be called. But before the Cops came, I talked to the young man.

I said…."Jason…..you are walking with the Devil." The boy looked at me and knew exactly what I meant. He put his head down. He said…"I'm sorry Coach…..I didn't think of it that way."

NEGATIVE FORCE is always out there trying to get us to do wrong things. It is all around us. Always was and always will be. We have to make a decision if we are going to let it affect us. It is our decision. *Doubt* is a key tool of the Devil. We are surrounded by people who constantly throw DOUBT our way. Instead of encouraging us….they give us DOUBT. Sometimes they use DOUBT in TRYING TO TAKE A DREAM AWAY.

Can you imagine how many times Mugsy Bogues was told he could never be a professional basketball player in the NBA at 5 foot 3 inches tall and 136 pounds. Can you imagine how many times his classmates at Dunbar High School in Baltimore, Maryland kidded him. Those people were helping the Devil by spreading DOUBT but good ole Mugsy had THICK SKIN and didn't let it stop him. He proved those people wrong and had a great career playing with the BIG boys in the National Basketball Association for 14 years.

He was POSITIVE MIND SET…SPECIAL MIND SET and did not allow NEGATIVE FORCE to take away his dreams. He DID NOT ALLOW THE ELEMENTS TO AFFECT HIS PERFORMANCE.

Here is another example for you.

Jim Abbott was born with only one arm. As a kid, like all kids, he wanted to play baseball. But wait a minute! How can you play baseball with only one arm? There was plenty of DOUBT to go around when he tried to play with his friends. He was the last guy chosen when his buddies would choose up sides to play a game.

What happened? He did NOT *allow the elements to affect his performance.* He became a pitcher. Yes, a pitcher and with only one arm. He was so good that he went to the University of Michigan and made their varsity baseball team. He went on after graduation to play in the major leagues with several teams. One year, with the New York Yankees, he threw a No-Hitter. The supreme accomplishment for a pitcher.

How's that for an example of overcoming NEGATIVE FORCE. This man demonstrated for all of us POSITIVE MIND SET...SPECIAL MIND SET.

He did not use EXCUSITIS. He not only became a DOMORE but he eventually became a HAVEMORE.

WOW! The Devil tried to ruin him but Jim Abbott beat the Devil. Jim Abbott was a General in GOD's Army. He was a TRUE *Devil Fighter!*

The Devils Auction- Author unknown

Here's a story for you. Several years ago one of the Big Devils of the world decided he was going to retire and he was going to have an auction of all his evil tools. He advertised all over the world. On the day of the auction……..devils came from all over the world. One by one….his tools of evil were sold off. Doubt was sold. Prejudice and Discrimination were sold. The list goes on and on. Finally one tool was left and the Devil said he was not going to auction off that last tool.

The other devils were angry. They traveled from all over the world and they wanted that tool. They complained and hollered… "sell that tool!"

The Devil said "nope…no way! "

Finally, when asked WHY he would not sell that last tool…. the Devil responded…. "If I ever decide to come out of retirement….it is the one tool that I will need to control every man, woman and child on the face of the earth." That tool was……………DISCOURAGEMENT!

Thus…………we are NOT allowed to get discouraged. We are NOT allowed to lose courage. If we do………..we walk with the Devil. We allow weakness to control us.

Remember…there are two types of life experiences….one type WE CONTROL and the other is experiences we do NOT CONTROL. The mind set of discouragement WE CONTROL.

No excuses…we are not allowed to get DISCOURAGED. This is a POSITIVE MIND SET that we have CONTROL of. A SPECIAL MIND SET……..not AVERAGE MIND SET! STRENGTH OVER WEAKNESS. Don't cheat our creator by being NEGATIVE.

We were not born with a label across our forehead saying…. "Hi….I'm going to be NEGATIVE". If we are NEGATIVE…..we put the label there….we put it there with our permission.

Enough said.

People are always looking for God-

Some people are always looking for God to come down from the sky and visit us.

NEGATIVE MIND SET people say….. "If there is a God how come he doesn't come down and show himself?"

Ah….the Devil at work using DOUBT.

The truth is, if we BELIEVE in a God…..then we understand that God is all around us. Look at the trees….the grass….the birds….the rivers…..see God. God made all there is…..right in front of our nose. You can even believe that God made the Devil to serve as a test for us. God gave us a brain. Now it is our decision how we use our brain….for good or evil. It is our choice. A LIFE EXPERIENCE THAT WE HAVE CONTROL OF. Ahhhhhh! Control! Remember what I said before…….experiences we have control of!

At the end of life on earth…..we all have to be accountable for what we do and what we didn't do. I believe this….do you? It all comes down to what you want to believe and for whatever reason. To me it is simple………POSITIVE MIND SET… SPECIAL MIND SET!

Chapter 9
Commitment and trust-

In developing POSITIVE MIND SET...SPECIAL MIND SET...the development and recognition of commitment and trust are BIG in importance.

So often AVERAGE MIND SET think that "small is Big." By this I mean that people have different perceptions of what a big commitment is. My idea of a great commitment may not be the same as what you believe a great commitment is. This happens very often when dealing with people and their definition or perception of a big commitment.

Check this out! Earlier in this book I discussed the following story and I explained how I tried to SELL....NOT TELL. I will talk about this story once again but this time I will discuss my comments about *Commitment* and developing *Trust*.

A few years back, we were in the middle of our off-season weight lifting program. The weight room was open four days a week and we were looking for players who would make a

GREAT commitment to the weight room and the off-season preparation. Remember... *"You have to pay the price."*

One of our players was going to the weight room only two days a week. The player thought he was making a great commitment by going two days. I discussed his commitment with him in a one on one meeting. I asked him if he was demonstrating AVERAGE or SPECIAL commitment. He looked at me sheepishly with his head down. I did not TELL him his commitment was average....I asked him a question that I already knew the answer to. He said...."I guess it is average....Coach".

I then asked him if his goal was to be AVERAGE or SPECIAL. Of course he answered........"SPECIAL".

I then asked him my patented question; "If you want to be SPECIAL....do you have to do AVERAGE things or SPECIAL things?" Again, the answer was obvious....an answer that I knew he would say....he uttered....."I have to do SPECIAL things. I need to be in the weight room four days."

Case closed.

I didn't have to TELL him, he TOLD himself. Or should I say....SOLD himself.

The cynic or NEGATIVE MIND SET person may say that the player just told me what I wanted to hear. Baloney! Now he said it, and I will hold him accountable if he doesn't follow his word. Here was a great example of communication and the concept...*sell...don't tell.*

We then talked about the DOMORE FAMILY. Do you Remember....the 3 major families of the world? We talked about the WISHMORE FAMILY and if we are to become one of the HAVEMORE FAMILY we have to first be a DOMORE. We talked about AVERAGE commitment and SPECIAL commitment. I was trying to sell him rather than tell him on his AVERAGE commitment in the weight room.

I wanted him to realize it himself. If he could understand that his commitment was not SPECIAL......and he was not really a DOMORE...he would come to realize that his commitment was AVERAGE.

With a greater commitment on his part, he would show that he was being a DOMORE. By being a DOMORE he was on his way to SPECIAL MIND SET.

We then talked about developing TRUST. He came to understand that the *more* commitment, the *more* trust in him by the coaching staff and his teammates. This was MOST important if he was to reach the personal and team goals that were set by him and his teammates.

The concept I was trying to sell was....... *"the greater the commitment...the greater the trust."*

Trust is a two way street-

Trust is a two way street. In relationships between people, TRUST is something that must be constantly developed and maintained.

A man and wife have to trust each other. There can be no "ands..ifs or buts" Divorces happen so often because TRUST has been destroyed.

A worker in the work place can not advance his position without developing a reputation as being a person you can have great TRUST in. TRUST is built on commitment. Thus COMMITMENT is evaluated by performance…. COMMITMENT leads to TRUST!

Do we do AVERAGE things or do we do SPECIAL things in our daily performance ….our daily commitment. The greater the commitment in a husband-wife relationship, the greater the TRUST.

The greater the commitment of the worker in his job, the higher level of TRUST in the worker. The supervisor can TRUST the worker. Thus the supervisor can give the worker bigger responsibilities. The worker now has a *better* chance to move up the ladder of success in the company.

TRUST equates to one's reputation. Reputation is our #1 asset in life….in any relationship.

Commitment and Trust go together as one! Earlier in this book I mentioned that I and my wife have been married for

50 years...... Did this happen by accident????? We have lasted because of Commitment and Trust!

Two Types of People when it comes to TRUST-

When it comes to GIVING TRUST, there are two types of people.

One type GIVES TRUST immediately. Upon meeting someone they will have a tendency to give TRUST "right now."

The other group, only give TRUST after a period of time. After the person to receive the TRUST proves themselves to be TRUSTWORTHY.

When a person is in a position of leadership they NEED to have their subordinates TRUST them immediately in order to have maximum productivity. He or she has to SELL the workers in their charge that they can be trusted 100%. This leader can not wait six months until his workers learn to TRUST him. TRUST of him has to happen quickly. For the sake of the success of the organization or a team, this TRUST of the leader is most important if the subordinates are to reach a level of maximum success....maximum productivity.

Thus, *it is a two way street.*

If the person in a leadership role EXPECTS his subordinates to TRUST him "right now"......he too must TRUST his people "right now". The leader must be the first type of

TRUST person mentioned above. He must give TRUST immediately.

POSITIVE MIND SET…SPECIAL MIND SET are strong to the point where they can give TRUST immediately.

In your development as a strong human being……GIVE TRUST "right now." If the person whom you are giving TRUST, *let's you down*….. "So what?" You have THICK SKIN. You did the RIGHT thing. The other person did the WRONG thing. You demonstrated POSITIVE MIND SET…SPECIAL MIND SET. The other person was weak and demonstrated NEGATIVE MIND SET…AVERAGE MIND SET.

When dealing with people….always remember the 90-10 rule. Unfortunately, 90 percent of people are in the AVERAGE MIND SET mode most of the time and *don't be surprised* if they misuse your TRUST in them.

Please remember what I said previously, AVERAGE MIND SET people are NOT bad people. The are our friends, relatives, neighbors, co-workers, etc.,. Nice people who just think AVERAGE. These same AVERAGE MIND SET people think nothing about destroying TRUST that people have in them. It happens all the time. It happens all around us. We see it every day.

Soooooooooooo….don't be surprised when people disappoint you. Chances are they do not even know that they are DOING just that….disappointing you and destroying the TRUST you gave them.

You, on the other hand, should be aware of this TRUST concept and *never Destroy* a TRUST. Never insult your name by doing so. Never brake your Honor Code which includes TRUST as a key component.

Chapter 10
Great Examples of POSITIVE MIND SET or NEGATIVE MIND SET

This chapter is dedicated to different experiences that I have had in the past. These stories have stayed with me through the years. I have used them to serve as examples of a specific MIND SET.

Don't marry a rich man!

Back in 1961, I was 24 years old and in my 3rd year of teaching and coaching. During the summer I got lucky and got a great summer job at the Silver Point Beach Club in Atlantic Beach, Long Island, New York. My job was to be Supervisor of Social Events and Sports Activities.

One day, an elderly grandmother came up to me and asked what activities I had for a young 13 year old girl. She looked and acted like a spirited lady and a fun type person.

I was in a good mood that day and I responded. "Well… we have a lot of 14 year old boys for her to make her acquaintance." She laughed and said…. "Oh, she has plenty of those already." I said… "Great….she will find a handsome rich guy….get married and live happily ever after." I was just being a wise guy. I could tell she was a fun person.

She popped up and said….. "Oh NO…..not good to get married to a rich man…..good to get married to a man who is going to be rich. This way they both travel the road to success together."

WOW! What a great lesson I just learned.

I always remembered this story and have told it often. It is a great example of SPECIAL MIND SET.

AVERAGE MIND SET is always looking for rich people to get married to. An age old name for these people is "Gold Diggers."

SPECIAL MIND SET is looking for a great person whom they can share great life experiences with.. In this way, they can develop a strong bond together because of their life experiences climbing the mountain together. In this way the marriage has a better chance for survival. They bond together. They live and struggle together through the good and the bad.

They can be DOMORES and then HAVEMORES together.

Two Feet On The Ground-

Maybe you've heard this one before. Years ago as a young man at the Beach Club I mentioned in the above story, I met a older man I am guessing was in his 80's. I was trying to be friendly and I asked him. " How are you sir?".   He said…." Young man…..everyday I get up and put two feet on the ground is a great day for me."

Ah…..another great lesson.   No complaining here by this old timer. He was POSITIVE MIND SET……SPECIAL MIND SET. This was another story that I have told to others through the years.

Racist generalities-

I mentioned earlier in this book this story……but I think it is work mentioning again to stress the WEAKNESS of RACIAL GENERALITIES.

In 1972 I was a teacher at Plainfield High School in Plainfield, New Jersey. One day, I was in the teachers room and a older female teacher came into the room complaining to other teachers that were present that "they" would not do this….. "they" would not do that…etc.,. The "they" she was referring to were black kids that we had in the school. I knew this to be a fact because all of the students were Black.

Another example of NEGATIVE FORCE.

I saw an opportunity to attack the Devil. I said… "What about Kevin Bowie?"

She said…. "Well…he's different."

I said…. "What about Nokey Johnson, Sam Davis, Sam Stepney, John Alexander?"

She said…. "Well they are different."

I said…… "Yes…..they are different." "They" are not all the same so don't make a generality. The teacher got angry with me and stormed out of the teachers room. I was pretty proud of myself. I attacked her ignorance…..a tool of the Devil as far as I was concerned.

I saw this type of behavior on her part as being NEGATIVE FORCE …AVERAGE MIND SET.

Remember, I was a kid that was born and raised in New York City, in Harlem and I learned from a young age that *all people were not the same.*

Judge People One at a Time-

My father, George Theodosatos was my first teacher. He was from Greece. He left home as a 12 year old boy in 1915 and became a merchant seaman. Many kids did this in the old days in Europe.

As a 17 year old, he jumped ship in Norfolk, Virginia and started his life in America. He could not speak a word of English. He did not have a cent in his pockets. He walked the streets of Norfolk trying to talk to people. He spoke with a woman who understood that he was talking Greek and she took him to a Greek man that she knew. The man owned a Candy and Ice Cream store and took my father under his wing. He gave him a job washing dishes and he taught him how to make candy and ice cream. My father later became a cook and later a Chef for a restaurant in New York City.

He never graduated from high school. He was self taught. He would sit at the kitchen table after he came home from work and take out the old encyclopedia. He would take the dictionary part and write 10 definitions of words 10 times each. He would write each word 100 times to learn spelling.

I always brag to people that my father got his college degree from the College of Living. He got his Masters Degree from the School of Hard Knocks. He got his Doctorate from the University of Hard Work.

He taught me many lessons but the two most important ones were ; …………..*that some people are good and some people are bad.* ………….*never insult your name*

He would say to me with his Greek accent…. "Milton…. some Jew no good….some Jew good……some colored no good…..some colored good people……some Italian good …some no good…some in mafia…no good…..etc.,etc."

He taught me that everyone had to be judged as *one individual*....... NOT as a group.   Without my knowing it…..my father was teaching me to be SPECIAL MIND SET.

He also taught me to *Never Insult My Name.*

I was about 9 years old and my mother took me to my father's restaurant for a visit one Saturday. My father gave me a treat……vanilla ice cream and chocolate syrup. I loved vanilla ice cream. All Kids do. One of my fathers customers came into the restaurant and sat down next to me. He knew I was my father's son. He said to me….. "You have a long last name….do you like having such a long name?" I said… "No" At this point my father reached across my table and cracked me across the face. He shouted….. "Shame on you…..never insult your name….the only thing a man has **is his name**. No money in all the world will take the place of your name. Never insult your name." You can bet your life I never knowingly tried to insult my name again. I still remember that crack across the face. Today, my father would probably be arrested for child abuse. But, I thank him for that lesson. I never changed my name or shortened my name as many Greek Americans have done who had long names. They shorten their names for convenience or so they would sound more American and not be discriminated against for whatever reason. I truly believe that this MIND SET helped me to develop that SPECIAL MIND SET attitude which I in turn would try teach others as the years would go by. It is a story I have told often to try and SELL the concept of SPECIAL MIND SET as compared to AVERAGE MIND SET.

Be a dreamer-

I was reading a story about Albert Einstein. He stressed a MIND SET concept that I always use in my discussions. Ole Al said…. *"Imagination is more important than intelligence."* WOW! Another great one!

Be a dreamer. Think big and if you fail….you fail high.

I always use the story of the great heavyweight fighters Muhammad Ali and Joe Frasier. In one of their fights, Joe Frasier lost. Students at the school I was teaching at, said…. "Ali kicked Joe Frasier's butt. Frasier lost." I interrupted them. I said… "Are you sure Frasier lost or did he come in second?" The students looked at me with puzzlement.

I stressed to the students that Winning is best. But losing in this case meant that Frasier failed high and received $5 million dollars for his failure. Frasier d*reamed* of winning but in the process failed….he failed high. If he never *dreamed* of winning, he would have never been in that fight with Ali. He would have never tried for *fear of failing*. Frasier *overcame the fear of failure*. Another great example of SPECIAL… POSITIVE MIND SET.

Reading is food for the mind-

John Wooten, the legendary basketball coach from UCLA spoke at a basketball clinic years ago and lectured on a great mind set concept. He said……. *"Reading is food for the mind."* He tried to sell this concept to his players. His goal was to help them make themselves better people. If they could make themselves better...stronger people....they would become SPECIAL MIND SET. Now they would have a better chance to be successful. Yes or No! Right or wrong? What do you think?

In my lectures I always use this story. I stress that we need food for both our body and mind. So often we eat the wrong foods....both for our body and our mind.

The $5 Doctor-

In 1998 I read a story in one of the local newspapers about an 85 year old Doctor who just died in Brooklyn, New York. The story went on to explain how this 85 year old Doctor was still making HOUSE CALLS at the age of 85. Something which is unheard of today....in these great modern times. His fee was only $5 for a house call. WOW! How is that for a bargain?

The article went on to explain that he made these house calls in a very bad neighborhood and many times he charged NOTHING.....ZERO....because the people could not afford to pay.

Now I ask you.......was this man a real hero? He wasn't a movie star. He wasn't an athlete. He wasn't a big shot celebrity. HE WAS BETTER.

He was an angel sent by our GOD! No doubt about it! He was very, very, very SPECIAL. A great example for all of us to remember.

A Warren Buffett Story

Not too long ago I watched a TV show where Warren Buffett was being interviewed. Buffett is one of the richest men in the world and I was interested in hearing some of thoughts.

When asked *Why he was giving away so much money to charities*....money that he worked hard for......He responded....and I am paraphrasing.....

"I never was a worker....I was a collector of money. People who work are factory workers....construction laborers. I never worked. I was a collector"

To me, this is SPECIAL MIND SET.

AVERAGE MIND SET thinking would say, "Yes, I worked hard and for many years for my money."

Here was a man that worth so much money and he was still able to not allow his success of making of money to NOT destroy in his mind....the TRUTH. Great SPECIAL MIND SET!

USA Hockey Vs. USSR

Do you remember the 1960 Winter Olympics when the USA Hockey Team upset the great USSR Team to Win the Gold Medal? Someone forgot to tell the Yanks they were suppose to lose!

Another great example of people who were able to be successful due to a SPECIAL MIND SET……..definitely NOT AVERAGE.

"Treat them like slaves"

Back in 1994 I was again teaching and coaching at an all black high school. I was having a conversation with one of the black coaches in the school about my leadership development program. I was stressing my attempt to develop leadership qualities in our young athletes. This particular black coach, and for obvious reasons I will not mention his name, tried to sell me on an idea. He tried to convince me that the best way to get black athletes to respond in a positive fashion was to "treat them like slaves." "Just tell them what to do"…… WOW…..I could not believe my ears. I could not believe that a black person would say such a thing. I responded by telling this man that his MIND SET was totally wrong. I can not and will not use the profanity words that I used to tell off this coach. I was really teed off to say the least. I attacked this NEGATIVE thinking. I saw it as a chance to fight the Devil. This was BULL_____!...You fill in the rest of the letters! It surprised me that this thinking would come from a black person.

A few months prior to this incident, I had another conversation with this black coach about the importance of a long Achilles tendon and how the long Achilles helps an athlete in speed and jumping ability. I related to him a story about Dr. Peter Karpovich and his teachings while I was a student of his at Springfield College in physiology of exercise class. Dr. Karpovich was world renown for his studies on the human body and the affects on athletic performance. The good Doctor had done studies on the Achilles tendon. He studied black and white athletes. He found that 80% of blacks had a long tendon while only 20% of white athletes had a long tendon. This was back in 1957.

The black coach I was telling this to said…. "NO..that's racist". I said…. "NO…that's science."

A couple of weeks went by and I was reading an article in a newspaper where Roger Banister, the first man to break the 4 minute mile, was being interviewed. Dr. Banister was asked why there were so many black athletes excelling in the sprints and jumping events in track and field. Dr. Banister answered….."It is probably NOT POLITICALLY CORRECT TO SAY….but it is because of the Achilles Tendon…etc.,etc.." I cut out the news article and showed it to the black coach. He was surprised…and said… 'Oh….I didn't know."

This was another example of how ignorance helps to create NEGATIVE FORCE……NEGATIVE MIND SET.

The Diner Story

Here is another story you will like.

Back in the 1970's..........I was in a Diner on Route 22 in North Plainfield, New Jersey. I was having a cup of coffee and a piece of apple pie. I was reading the morning newspaper. In the booth next to me were two couples. People who were probably in their early 40's. They were talking about Muhammad Ali and black fighters. One man said to the other; "You can't hit them in the head….they have a thicker head than whites. You have to hit them in the stomach…they have weak stomachs. You can take a baseball bat and hit them in the head and they won't feel it" WOW!......

I wanted to get up and hit that guy on the side of the head. What a jerk! I couldn't believe what I was hearing.

Another example of unbelievable ignorance.

Black Quarterbacks

Here is another.

As a coach of black players I had several excellent quarterbacks and offensive centers. Back in the 1970's and 1980's and even in later years, I tried to sell college recruiters on these players. I met with resistance. I was told they were not smart enough. Quarterbacks had to think. Offensive Centers had to read defenses and make line calls. They had to think.

WOW....more ignorance. MORE NEGATIVE FORCE. Luckily today....we see many teams that have black Quarterbacks and Offensive Centers. So things have become better in that regard.

The World Basketball Championships

Here is yet another story......more up to date.

The date is August 31, 2006. The situation is as follows. The World Basketball Championships in Saitama, Japan The Semi Finals between The USA and Greece. Final Score......
Greece 101
USA   95

What happened?????????? Impossible......this can't happen!

The USA team made up of super stars from the National Basketball Association....the pros....supposedly the best players in the world, or so we are told by the media. A team made up of players getting millions and millions of dollars. The highest paid players in the world. They had a coach many considered the best in the world. Players that came from a country of over 300 million people. A team that was predicated to Win the championship.

The team from Greece was not ranked at all. They were players from a country of 10 million people. How much do they get paid????? What is the name of their coach???? They had no chance to win....right? Someone forgot to tell those Greeks. After all, they are all white players playing against a USA team of almost all black players. And...they can't jump.... remember the movie "White Men Can't Jump".

Well, I dare say that the MIND SET of these Greek players and their coaches were of a very SPECIAL MIND SET. This was a great victory over the weakness of GENERALITIES and WRONG PERCEPTIONS.

Mules

Another story…last but not least in this chapter. Years ago I am having a conversation with an old friend who is coaching in the National Football League. He is relating to me a conversation he had with one of the owners of one of the teams. The owner was telling my friend that he only wanted black players. The owner said that white players think too much. Black players are better…..they are "mules". WOW…… How is that for NEGATIVE FOOD…..NEGATIVE FORCE….. WEAKNESS……..

Do you think the Devil was sitting in that owner's house. I think so! Stories like this convinced me of the need and importance of my developing a MIND SET program for my athletes. I had to try and fight this weakness of our society. WEAKNESS OF MISINFORMATION….. WEAKNESS OF GENERALITIES…….WEAKNESS OF IGNORANCE…. WEAKNESS OF NEGATIVE FORCE…….

Chapter 11
Competitors are Made Not Born- and Overcoming the Fear of Failure

Competitors are MADE not born. So often we hear the statement…. "he was born a competitor"…or "he was a born whatever." This way of thinking, I believe to be incorrect. People learn to be competitors or they learn to NOT compete. This is where one of the most important skills we have to learn pops up.

OVERCOMING THE FEAR OF FAILURE.

From the day we are born we gradually learn that FAILURE is bad. And……we learn that the only way to NOT fail is to NOT TRY. If we do not TRY something….how can we fail? Simple. Live in mediocrity….weakness…AVERAGE MIND SET….NEGATIVE MIND SET and we can never fail. We also can never taste the fruits of great success if we escape from challenges and high goals.

Great athletes and anyone who strives for great success have to learn to OVERCOME THE FEAR OF FAILURE.

In the past I have used the example of the Gladiator in the Arena. He is the competitor. He will live or die. He has everything to gain or lose. The person who sits in the Gallery wins or loses nothing. They can either clap or boo the competitor in the Arena. And so it is with life. The competitors get the riches or the boos. It goes with the territory….one or the other. When we learn to OVERCOME THE FEAR OF FAILURE we demonstrate great strength…..POSITIVE MIND SET….SPECIAL MIND SET.

Fear can be both good and bad. Fear can motivate us to succeed…..to keep trying….to not give up. Fear can help us develop into a POSITIVE MIND SET……SPECIAL MIND SET person.

Fear on the other hand, can make us weak. Fear can keep us in the AVERAGE MIND SET…NEGATIVE MIND SET MODE for an entire lifetime.

So FEAR can be considered a NEGATIVE or a POSITIVE……Remember the concept….. *"Take a negative and turn it into a positive."* Thus FEAR is good for the person who will use it to help himself succeed. The POSITIVE MIND SET…SPECIAL MIND SET person will use FEAR to their advantage.

FEAR gets the adrenalin flowing. Adrenalin gets the juices moving and we either RUN AWAY from the challenge (as in NEGATIVE MIND SET…AVERAGE MIND SET) or the juices get us moving TOWARDS the challenge. ATTACK the challenge....don't run away.

This my friend is POSITIVE MIND SET...SPECIAL MIND SET.

"The will to win is not nearly as important as the will to prepare to win-" - Bobby Knight

Everyone wants to WIN! But....But....But.....are you willing to pay the price to win????? So, when I find people who say.... "Yes....I want to win," this means very little to me. The real thing I am looking for is if the person is *willing to pay the price*. Talk is cheap. Thus only by effort and performance, and commitment can I evaluate if a person is really *willing to prepare to win*.

It is characteristic of NEGATIVE MIND SET...AVERAGE MIND SET people to pay a *limited* price for an attempt at success. Their perception of BIG is SMALL. Their mind is full of the words....I DID ENOUGH...and ...I CAN"T. Very seldom do they consider being a DOMORE.

It is characteristic of POSITIVE MIND SET...SPECIAL MIND SET people to NOT EVER SAY..... "I did enough or I can't" They are always trying to DOMORE.

All people want to be successful. But *not all people want to pay the price THAT IS NECESSARY* to reach the level of success they want.

People must first move from the WISHMORE family to the DOMORE family. Then, after years of tremendous effort and tremendous commitment and great investment, the person has a chance to become a HAVEMORE family member.

We all start off with a AVERAGE MIND SET. We learn to be NEGATIVE MIND SET. Then we have to unlearn the negative lessons we learned. Thus we can make ourselves better and become POSITIVE MIND SET...SPECIAL MIND SET.

But in order for this to happen, we must understand that there is a difference between POSITIVE AND NEGATIVE and AVERAGE AND SPECIAL MIND SET. And more importantly......we must understand that we *learned* to be the way we are. We were not born with a label across our forehead saying

…….. "Hi…….I'm going to be AVERAGE."

"The Race if very seldom won
by the front runner."
___

Through the years I have had many opportunities to talk with parents about their children. Parents whose children were not progressing at the level or rate that the parents wanted and expected. They were not happy with the progress of their children….be it in school work or in behavior.

In my talk with parents I always tried to SELL them on two ideas.

Number one…… I tried to SELL parents *to not beat themselves up.* Parents in our country have been programmed to believe that they are responsible for ALL the failures of their kids. *Baloney!* I tried to SELL the parents that there are many, many factors that affect our children. Everything from peer pressure, parents, society, other family members and heredity. YES, heredity. The SEED. The LUCK of the DRAW, so to speak.

Too little is mentioned about this key factor.

When I used to teach senior health (it was called Family Living), I taught physical and mental health, drug education, career planning, goal setting, sex education and Money Management, just to mention a few of the interesting and meaningful areas of concern.

I would ask the students to raise their hands when they agreed to the following four questions; I would ask my classes;

How many of you know GOOD people who came from GOOD families? Everyone would raise their hand.

How many of you know BAD people who came from GOOD families? Everyone would raise their hand.

How many of you know GOOD people who came from BAD families? Again, everyone would raise their hand.

And finally I would ask…..How many of you know BAD people who came from BAD families? Again, all students would raise their hand.

The moral of the story here is……so who is to blame? …or who is to get the credit? People have to be held accountable for their OWN actions and NOT blame others….especially their parents. I have seen many, many kids who were great who came from a family situation where you would guess that they would grow up to be a disaster. I have seen many kids come from great families who were just plan BAD. I call this a BAD SEED.

Soooooooo! I always tried to SELL parents to NOT be too hard on themselves.

The Number two point I tried to SELL parents on was….. *"Very seldom is the race won by the front runner."*

Have you ever been to the races? You know…the ponies! I love the races and have enjoyed many a day at the races. VERY SELDOM does the horse who takes the lead at the beginning of the race end up winning. The winner usually comes out of the pack. AND so it is with people.

More often the most successful people come from the middle of their high school class. In fact, to be the school valedictorian may be the KISS OF DEATH.

Every parent, including myself, would love for their kid to be the valedictorian. Unfortunately most parents feel that their children could have been more successful in school. I used to have my Health Class students bring in health articles from the local newspapers. We would discuss these articles every Friday. They were very, very interesting and informative. On several occasions, through the years, I had a student bring in an article about parents saying in surveys that if they had to do it over again, they would not have children. WOW! What a terrible thing! These parents were disappointed by how their children developed.

The MIND SET these parents needed …to help their children… was to STAY POSITIVE. Encourage their children. Don't give up on them. AND, remember, *"the race is very seldom won by the front runner."* Their child can develop into an outstanding success as the child GROWS up. Some people develop sooner than others, both physically and mentally.

The parents who are NEGATIVE MIND SET….AVERAGE MIND SET, will have a tendency to give up on their kids. They will feel bad. They will make excuses for their children (Sound familiar? EXCUSITIS). They will PUSH their kids DOWN instead of PUSHING them UP. In many situations, the parents and the children have a parting of the ways.

Remember…IT IS ALWAYS ABOUT OURSELVES. Thus when a child is doing poorly in either school work or behavior, the parents sees this problem as a reflection on them. Many parents….good people, who really tried all the POSITIVE things, end up BEATING THEMSELVES UP because of the results of their children.

POSITIVE MIND SET…SPECIAL MIND SET parents understand all of the factors that will MAKE their children what they will be.

COMPETITORS are made, not born. Children who start off the race in last place do not have to end up a loser. They can come from *way* behind and WIN the race.

It is all in the mind!   In the MIND SET!

Chapter 12
Expectations

Expectations is a word often used in the business word….or in the field of education. It is an idea loaded with NEGATIVE FORCE. It is a word thrown around recklessly…. in this guy's opinion. It is a dangerous word and in many cases it is a word that has *destroyed p*eople. Before an effort is ever given by SOME people, they have an EXPECTATION of success or failure. This can be very dangerous.

I say it is dangerous because the person having an expectation of failure ……a NEGATIVE result…… will not try to achieve a specific goal.

Expect to fail and you will! It happens more often than not. The person says…. "I thought it wouldn't work!" Failure was in their mind before the event took place. I say this is NEGATIVE MIND SET…AVERAGE MIND SET.

POSITIVE MIND SET…SPECIAL MIND SET… understands that success or failure can happen and they TRY anyway…. because it is the thing to do. The challenge is at hand and it is necessary….it is the correct thing to do….it is right to try and overcome the challenge.

Am I making this sound too complicated??? I hope not!

In the field of education, students are given National Tests in their early years and they are labeled. EXPECTATIONS are assumed of these children by their teachers and administrators. The Educators say….. "Well this student is a ……whatever!" Average Student…..Bright Student…..Slow Student.

WHAT A MISTAKE!

Students can feel this EXPECTATION by how the teacher acts towards them. The classmates pick up on this also. Now….the student goes through his school years with these EXPECTATIONS by his peers and his teachers. As a teacher of 31 years I was appalled by these expectations especially when certain students were EXPECTED to be slow students academically.

"Oh….he is not very smart"

"Oh…what do you expect…look at the home he comes from"

"She doesn't get any support at home about her school work"

"His test scores are very low."

The list of NEGATIVE MIND SET statements of expectations about students goes on and on. The great teachers are those who do NOT ACCEPT the idea of low EXPECTATIONS.

Back in 1965 I had a young man that was a senior in the high school I was teaching at and he wanted to go to college. He did not have very good grades and his SAT score was very low. There was no way he was going to be accepted in any of the colleges in the Northeast because his scores were too low and he could not make minimum standards for acceptance.

I knew this young man to be a great competitor. Someone who never gave up when he played for me on the gridiron. He was a hard worker and a young man of great character. BUT….BUT….he had low scores and the EXPECTATION was that he could never get into a college or if he got into a college, he would never graduate.

His Guidance Counselor, a nice lady but a AVERAGE MIND SET person, told me …. "he will never get into a college and if he ever did….he would never graduate."

Well. Needless to say, this motivated me. I knew that if this young man could ever get into a college he could make it based on his attitude and MIND SET. I found a small college in the Midwest. The requirements for admission were only a high school diploma. The college was easy to get into BUT he would have to still do satisfactory work to stay in school and to eventually graduate. They would give students a CHANCE. This young man DID graduate from this small college even though it took him five years instead of four years to get through. He ended up being a teacher in upstate New York. I do not want to mention his name or his high school for obvious reasons. But, those of his classmates who may end up reading this book will know who he is.

This was an example where I and this young man did not let LOW EXPECTATIONS stop the both of us from accomplishing a goal.

WE BEAT THE SYSTEM. THE SYSTEM STINKS!

Another great story. This time it is about a black youngster who was a member of my football team. He was a real fighter….a great competitor. His Guidance Counselor in school tried to convince his mother to send him to school to be a cook. Well, being a cook is OK….but he wanted to go to college and study business and play college football if that was possible. I taught him to DREAM and all my boys are DREAMERS. I knew that he if got a chance, he would make it.

We found a college down south that gave him a chance. He graduated in four years and today is a successful business man on Long Island.

This was another example of how we attacked the NEGATIVE FORCE of LOW EXPECTATIONS and we WON.

What kind of MIND SET do you think this was????????

Anyone Can WIN!

Forget LOW EXPECTATIONS.

The only EXPECTATIONS that are necessary are HIGH EXPECTATIONS FOR EVERYONE.

DON'T WORRY ABOUT FAILING. LET THE IDEA OF FAILING BE FOR THOSE TIMID SOULS THAT CHOOSE TO BE WEAK….NEGATIVE MIND SET…. AVERAGE MIND SET.

I say that there is no such thing as a dumb kid (I am not counting someone who was born retarded). There are only DUMB TEACHERS who do not know how to communicate and motivate and search for the Hot Button which will get a student to believe in themselves. This I believe with a PASSION.

Does it sound like I am attacking teachers? Well……. remember the 90-10 Rule! I dare say that 90% of the teachers I came in contact with were AVERAGE MIND SET. Remember what I said previously…….they can be nice people….but nonetheless….AVERAGE MIND SET and they fall into the trap of EXPECTATIONS and do a disservice to the students in their charge.

Yes, there are some who are born with MORE natural intelligence than others. We have tests for IQ but we DO NOT HAVE ANY TESTS FOR….. COMMON SENSE. There are many so called intelligent people who are stupid…. just watch TV….read the newspapers….if you do not believe me. NEGATIVE MIND SET…AVERAGE MIND SET is loaded with so called smart people who because of weakness of personality are dumb regardless of what their IQ scores say.

On the other hand...POSITIVE MIND SET...SPECIAL MIND SET people are full of people who cross the range of different levels of so called intelligence. I suggest to the experts that they come up with tests for evaluating levels of Common Sense and MIND SET. Now, that would be interesting.

"It's run it's course"

Here is a beautiful statement. Again, I am being a wise guy!

So often I have heard people say that something, "has run it's course." They are referring to a fad or a type of business...or whatever.

Let me give you an example. Not too long ago I heard a media person talking about the low attendance at arena 2 Professional football games. He stressed that at the beginning, people were interested because arena football was something NEW. Now, it is not new anymore and attendance has dropped off.

Here is how I read this type of thinking. The media person talking is blaming the low attendance on the fact that the game is not new anymore. He has developed an EXPECTATION that in the future, the attendance at games will be low because of the reason already mentioned. In his mind....he EXPECTS. Thus, when this media person talks to Management of a specific team about attendance and he gives his opinion (which is really worth zero)..... he is giving NEGATIVE FOOD…..NEGATIVE FORCE to Management.

Instead he could and should have been OPTIMISTIC about the future and GIVEN POSITIVE FORCE by giving reasons why and how the attendance could be increased. I repeat…. he should have said….WHY and HOW attendance could be Increased.

Such as…..get new…better….more exciting players….maybe a new coach is necessary…..maybe the front office with sales…. can re-organize and increase productivity. Maybe you have to fire some lazy workers. Maybe…hire additional sales people for ticket sales to increase attendance. Maybe Management should evaluate all phases of their product…. including Give-aways…sponsorship…..advertising etc.

Instead, the Media person had a simple NON PRODUCTIVE…NEGATIVE statement to make…."The game has run it's course in this town."

WOW! What NEGATIVITY. What kind of MIND SET is this???????

How come the New York Yankees don't say that baseball in New York has *run it's course?*

A few years ago, attendance in Major League Baseball was off and several teams were losing money and there was great concern about the so called National Pastime. Instead of quitting….giving up…..teams reorganized all phases of their business and today attendance is better than it has ever been.

"It's run it's course" is NEGATIVE MIND SET…. To use this EXCUSE….allows management to have a built-in excuse all set up…all ready to be used….. if failure occurs. EXPECTATION is FAILURE!

AVERAGE MIND SET ALL THE WAY!

Chapter 13
The Football Bible

Through the years I have accumulated poems, phrases, statements made by historians, philosophers, writers, poets, business people, clergy, Statesmen, coaches and teachers plus others. I have put these great lessons in a pamphlet form and called it my Football Bible.

When I was in sales, both with insurance and securities, I had a team of sale people under my wing. To motivate and encourage POSITIVE MIND SET.....SPECIAL MIND SET...I also used this BIBLE with them.

The BIBLE consists of hundreds of axioms, phrases and statements. In this chapter I will only stress some of these valuable lessons.

Some of the phrases have been mentioned earlier in this book but I will have some fun in this chapter as I bring these important lessons to you.

Heeeerre we go!

1. No one cheats you out of success except yourself.

A POSITIVE MIND SET...SPECIAL MIND SET person will never blame others for his or her lack of success. AVERAGE MIND SET behavior blames others....point fingers......they say.. "it was not my fault." " I didn't have an opportunity" SPECIAL MIND SET people create and find their own opportunities.

2. The future belongs to those who prepare for it. - Malcolm X

This concept goes along with CHALLENGES AND SOLUTIONS. No Excusitis. Make a plan. If it doesn't work.....make a new plan. Simple and complex as that. Keep climbing the mountain. SPECIAL MIND SET prepare for the future. SPECIAL MIND SET understands that the greatest plans made for the future will NOT work out on many occasions. Adjustments have to be made and the fight must be continued.

3. You play a game like you practice.

This goes back to…. "the will to win is not nearly as important as the will to prepare to win." Do you invest 25 cents or $25,000. The bigger the COMMITMENT the bigger the potential reward. NEGATIVE MIND SET...AVERAGE MIND SET do just enough (in their mind) to get it done. POSITIVE MIND SET….SPECIAL MIND SET extend themselves….they are a member of the DOMORE FAMILY.

The phrase **GOOD ENOUGH** is used often by AVERAGE MIND SET people when attempting a difficult task. "Enough" implies just getting by……and "Good" is short of best. So GOOD ENOUGH doesn't cut the mustard, so to speak……it is characteristic of AVERAGE MIND SET.

4. If you don't believe in yourself….
   no one else will.

POSITIVE MIND SET….SPECIAL MIND SET have learned to believe in themselves by OVERCOMING THE FEAR OF FAILURE. They understand that before others can believe in them, they MUST first believe in themselves. They DO NOT use such words as…. "I did enough"…or "I can't". They BELIEVE.

Remember……CAN'T MEANS ……WON'T. The man who says "I can't" do something…….changes his mind quickly when I say to him….. "How about I give you $1,000,000 to try?"….He quickly says….. "Oh….that's different…..for 1 million dollars, you bet your life I can do it."

5. The weakest guy in the world
   is the guy who alibis.

Here we go again. EXCUSITIS….by the weak. Certainly not POSITIVE MIND SET ….SPECIAL MIND SET behavior. NEGATIVE MIND SET…AVERAGE MIND SET people have trained themselves to accept quitting as being OK. They love the words; "I did enough" or "I can't". How do you rate yourself in this area of alibis and excuses? Can you get better in this important characteristic

6. The test of a person is the fight they make.

When we OVERCOME THE FEAR OF FAILURE and go into the POSITIVE MIND SET...SPECIAL MIND SET mode....we learn to continue the struggle....we continue the climb up the mountain....we fight on. It is easy to continue the journey when there is no resistance....but it shows character when a person continues the journey against the current...against the wind.....against the NEGATIVE forces that will occur. It is easy to separate the AVERAGE MIND SET and SPECIAL MIND SET people by watching the FIGHT THEY MAKE.

7. It is characteristic of weak people to AVOID challenges....of strong people to MEET challenges.

POSIITIVE MIND SET...SPECIAL MIND SET people LOVE challenges. It is a part of the excitement of living. They learn to be "problem solvers." They build great self-esteem, thus take on big challenges and if they FAIL......they FAIL HIGH.

8. The athlete competes in front of thousands of fans......his soul is stripped naked. The whole world sees what he or she is. Their character can NOT hide.

POSITIVE MIND SET...SPECIAL MIND SET...love to be in the arena. They learn to autograph their work with excellence. They strive to never insult their name. *This* attribute separates them from NEGATIVE MIND SET... AVERAGE MIND SET.

9. We can learn from athletes on this one.......

The demands on athletes are UN-NATURAL. There are NO MAKE-UP TESTS. IMMEDIATE RESULTS ARE REQUIRED.

WOW' Better get out of the kitchen if it is too hot! Once again, the POSITIVE MIND SET...SPECIAL MIND SET person is in the arena. No make up tests HERE means NO EXCUSITIS. No second chance on that day. In life we have only one life to live. We better do it right because there are NO REPLAYS…..NO MAKE UP TESTS. Autograph your work with excellence.

10. Eagles fly where others dare not!

Sparrows fly in herds or flocks or schools! Which is the right word? I am sure you get the message. POSITIVE MIND SET...SPECIAL MIND SET people are Eagles. Be an EAGLE! EAGLES go where others dare not. Thus they gain the fruits that others...the NEGATIVE MIND SET... AVERAGE MIND SET will never experience.

In which world do you want to live?

The world of the EAGLES or the world of the SPARROWS?

11. Every job is a self portrait of the person who did it.

This is a great one.

NEGATIVE MIND SET...AVERAGE MIND SET will be content to just do a mediocre job. To just get by. To just do enough.

POSITIVE MIND SET...SPECIAL MIND SET people have a great NEED to autograph their work with excellence. They do not want to insult their name. They want to be SPECIAL and NOT AVERAGE. They know that to develop a great reputation they have to earn it through hard and long work....though great commitment. They will not allow a NEGATIVE effort hurt their reputation which they worked so hard to develop.

12. Vince Lombardi...the great football coach and his great talk about;

What it takes to be No. 1

Coach Lombardi goes on to explain, "Winning is not a sometime thing; it's an all time thing. You don't do things right once in awhile, you do them right all of the time." Here is where we stress that POSITIVE MIND SET... SPECIAL MIND SET people separate themselves from NEGATIVE MIND SET...AVERAGE MIND SET people by autographing their work with excellence *ALL OF THE TIME.*

13. Dare Greatly...

...the poem by the late and great President Teddy Roosevelt.

> "It is not the critic who counts, nor the man who points out how the strong man tumbled,
>
> Or where the doer of deeds could have done better,
>
> The credit belongs to the man who is actually in the arena, whose face is marred by dust and sweat and blood, who strives valiantly,
>
> Who errs and comes up short again and again,
>
> Who knows the great enthusiasms, the great devotions and spends himself in a worthy cause,
>
> Who at the best knows in the end the triumph of high achievement, and who at the worst if he fails at least fails while DARING GREATLY,
>
> So that his place shall never be with those cold and timid souls who know neither victory or defeat."

WOW! Does this say it all? The competitor is in the arena NOT the gallery. The DOMORE family person who has to overcome the FEAR OF FAILURE. The EAGLE who experiences great rewards and who goes where others dare NOT. The POSITIVE MIND SET...SPECIAL MIND SET person who if he is to fail, fails high. This poem is a great one!!!!!!

14. Champions Creed

I am not judged by the number of times

I have failed…

I am not judged by the number of times

I have succeeded….

But I am judged by the number of times that

I have failed and kept trying.

Author Unknown

NEGATIVE MIND SET…..AVERAGE MIND SET folks may not understand these words. POSITIVE MIND SET…SPECIAL MIND SET folks understand that failing is NOT important. To continue the climb up the mountain is the only thing that is important. To continue……to continue…….to continue! The real fun is in the journey. The climb up the mountain.

15. Be a Thoroughbred

You enter this world naked and bare…

You go through life with worry and care….

Then you die….and know not where….but don't despair…. because if you are a Thoroughbred here…..you'll be a Thoroughbred there.

Now….you all go out and be a Thoroughbred!

Author Unknown

Another great one! Your goal is to be either AVERAGE OR SPECIAL. What is your choice? You have one of two choices. Actually…..you only have one choice. SPECIAL……………..

16. This is another great one we have learned from the world of athletics.

"As long as the coach shouts at you, you know that he is interested in you. When he doesn't ever say a word to you…. chances are he doesn't even know you are around."

POSITIVE MIND SET…SPECIAL MIND SET people learn to do the following;

1. Love criticism.
2. Have thick skin as compared to thin skin.
3. Be grateful for the concern of the person giving the criticism.
4. Take this somewhat negative and turn it into a positive.
5. Learn from the criticism.
6. Strive to be a DOMORE family member.

Only the gamefish swim upstream….the weak are content to stay where they are. Another great trait of POSITIVE MIND SET…SPECIAL MIND SET.

Are you a gamefish?

17. Cowards can fight when they are ahead….but coming from behind shows who the individual really is!

NEGATIVE MIND SET…AVERAGE MIND SET are tough when they are ahead. When they get behind in a game or in life, they quit and resign from effort. They GIVE UP. How many people do you know that have GIVEN UP on life already? They do not understand the wonderful gift of life they have received. Many of these people who have GIVEN UP are young people and this is a real tragedy of our society.

In my years as a teacher and coach, I have seen 15 and 16 year old kids who have GIVEN UP on life. This condition always motivated me to continue the fight of trying to change their MIND SET. This fight, I always believed, was my way of giving back to my creator who gave me life and life experiences which helped me develop my MIND SET and this program.

18. In football we say….

"It is not a sin to get blocked….it is a sin to remain blocked"

In life it is not a sin to make a "so called mistake"…..it is a sin to allow that mistake from allowing you to continue your effort. POSITIVE MIND SET…SPECIAL MIND SET…know that they will make many so called mistakes.

So what?

Make a new decision and move on. Continue the effort. DON'T ALLOW THE ELEMENTS TO AFFECT YOU IN A NEGATIVE WAY.

19. The fun is in the battle.

POSITIVE MIND SET…SPECIAL MIND SET love the battle. They love to be problem solvers. In fact, they look for problems to solve. They live life to the fullest. To be in the battle is to be in the arena. There is no fun in the gallery. Join the FUN! Join the FIGHT! Join the BATTLE!

20. The best players help others to be best players.

POSITIVE MIND SET…SPECIAL MIND SET people LEAD. They strive to LEAD. They step forward and take on new responsibilities. NEGATIVE MIND SET…AVERAGE MIND mode strives to escape from responsibilities. In the business world…they might say; "that's not my job" or "I don't get paid to do that." In sports, the best athlete may not be the BEST player. The BEST player is the player who is a POSITIVE LEADER. One who makes the people around him BETTER. That's the BEST PLAYER.

21. A person's life is what his thoughts make of it. Be a dreamer. And If you can IMAGINE it, you can ACHIEVE it. If you can DREAM it, you can BECOME it.

Albert Einstein said…. "imagination is more important than intelligence."

In other words…..be a dreamer. Dream of doing great things. This dreaming means that you will have to have high goals. Failure may occur. So what? If you are a POSITIVE MIND SET…SPECIAL MIND SET person you love the challenge. You love to be a problem solver. You have thick skin. You can overcome the fear of failure.

One of the greatest speeches ever made was by Martin Luther King when he said…. "I have a dream…etc.,." WOW…. what a POSITIVE MIND SET…SPECIAL MIND SET.

For every great discovery that was ever made in all of history, first there was a dream.

22. This is one of the greatest laws of the universe. "If you think in negative terms, you will get negative results. If you think in positive terms, you can get positive results. Only by believing can you succeed."   Author Unknown

---

How often have you heard a person say; "I can't." Usually, CAN'T means WON'T. How about if I offered the person who said CAN'T….$1,000,000 to try? WOW! You would see how fast that person changes their mind. "Well that's different…..I certainly will try."..says our CAN'T person. When you hear the word CAN'T……you know where the MIND SET of that person is.

Everything in life has a WEIGHT to it. Another word would be VALUE. We can and CAN'T do things based on our value system. The value systems of AVERAGE MIND SET and SPECIAL MIND SET is quite different to say the least.

When we are in a POSITIVE MIND SET…SPECIAL MIND SET mode….we do not live in the CAN'T WORLD.

23. Our doubts are traitors to us….. They make us lose the will to try…. They force us to NOT attempt…. Courage and self-discipline will overcome this weakness of the human spirit. Author Unknown

DOUBT is one of the main tools of the Devil. Remember him? Yes, that's right…..the guy who is always trying to make us weak. When we live in the NEGATIVE MIND SET… AVERAGE MIND SET mode we are full of *DOUBT*. Be a Thoroughbred NOT an old nag! Don't confuse DOUBT with being cautious. It is wise to be cautious in many situations. But, when we let being cautious turn into DOUBT, then we live in the NEGATIVE MIND SET…AVAREGA MIND SET mode.

24. If I remember correctly, it was Robert Kennedy who said;

"Some people see things and say WHY?....some people dream of things and say WHY NOT?

Remember what Albert Einstein said….."Be a dreamer."… This is POSITIVE MIND SET…SPECIAL MIND SET.

Some people blame circumstances for what they are or don't have….Some people look for the circumstances and things they want and if they can't find them…..THEY MAKE THEM.

The Legendary warrior Hannibal, as he charged through conquering lands said…… "We will find a way…or we will make a way." A great example of POSITIVE MIND SET… SPECIAL MIND SET.

We live in a world today where almost everyone has a built in EXCUSE for failure. The disease EXCUSITIS. It appears that we are all VICTIMS of something and thus we have built- in excuses for anticipated failure….. instead of looking in the mirror and seeing the person who has CONTROL.

Remember the concept….Two types of Life Experiences. Those we have control over and those we have no control over.

WE ARE IN CHARGE. Make a decision…… NEGATIVE OR POSITIVE ……AVERAGE OR SPECIAL MIND SET.

In my 47 years of teaching and coaching and 70 years of living, I have heard countless numbers of people who complained….. "My daddy wasn't rich so I couldn't go to college"….. "I came from a broken home"…… "I had this excuse or I had that excuse." Excuses….Excuses. This type of attitude definitely separates the AVERAGE AND SPECIAL MIND SET folks.

As a teacher and coach I had opportunity to talk with many young people who came from single family homes. In some cases the person had no parents and lived with a grand-mother or a foster home. I would have one on one talks with these students and players to try and find out about future goals, aspirations, family background, etc., etc. I would try to get information that would help me try to find the individual's HOT BUTTON. If I could find their HOT BUTTON, then I had a greater chance to communicate with that person and hopefully say and do something that would help that person MAKE THEMSELVES A BETTER PERSON …a STRONGER PERSON.

I would always ask the question mentioned above;

"Do you live with your Mom and Dad?" Then they would say whether or not it was with Mom and Dad or just Mom or just Grandmom etc.,. If they said they live with just their Mom or Grandmom or a Foster home, I would say to the person…

"Great….you are lucky….tell me why!"

They would look at me in amazement. They would say… "Coach, I thought it was better to come from a two parent home." I would respond… "Yes, we all know that it *should* be better to come from a two parent home. But, who probably has a more difficult…harder time growing up?"

"You or the guy with two parents?" The student would respond, "I do!" Then I would hit them with…… "By the time you are 30 years old, your life experiences were harder than the guy with two parents. If you did it right…..the person who traveled the more difficult road should be the stronger person….Right or Wrong?"

Aw…..TAKE A NEGATIVE AND TURN IT INTO A POSITIVE.

NO EXCUSES.

GET IT DONE!!!!!

Don't live the life of a VICTIM.

25. The guy who gets AHEAD is the guy who does more

(aw….a DOMORE)

The guy who gets ahead is the guy who does more *than is necessary and keeps doing it*. Add to this what the great Michigan State coach Duffy Daugherty said…. "The difference between good and great is just a little extra effort. Another example of the DOMORE family. POSITIVE MIND SET…SPECIAL MIND SET. DOMORE Baby………DO MORE!

26. Commitment will cost you!

Using the 90-10 rule, 90% of the people live most of the time in the AVERAGE MIND SET mode. To DOMORE is not what they want to do. God forbid they do more! They want to get home after work. They want to party. They want to see their friends. They do not want to give up their free time. They do not want to give up entertainment. God forbid they should stay late at work and increase their commitment….they may get a promotion because they acted SPECIAL. WOW! I am being a Wise Guy! By making a greater commitment they may not have an excuse for failure. I am being facetious but I think you get the message.

Remember…..the more commitment, the more trust earned, the more chance for getting added responsibilities, the more chance for advancement. This equates to more work. WHAT! MORE WORK! Who wants more work????? I don't want more work….I want less work!

Ha..Ha…Am I being a wise guy????

Remember…AVERAGE MIND SET thinks WORK is a bad word. Remember….SPECIAL MIND SET thinks WORK is a GREAT WORD. What do you think??????????????????

27. Great leaders do not try to get people to look up to them, but rather great leaders try to get people to believe MORE in themselves.

In other words….PUSH PEOPLE UP.

Be POSITIVE MIND SET …SPECIAL MIND SET.

Do you want people to like you better?

Do you want people to respect you more?

Do you want people to believe in you?

Do you want people to TRUST you more?

Do you want to demonstrate leadership qualities?

Then PUSH PEOPLE UP.

28. The poem DON'T EVER QUIT…..

Live this poem and you will live in the world of …… POSITIVE MINDSET…SPECIAL MIND SET.

Amen!

DON"T EVER QUIT

When things go wrong, as they sometimes will,
When the road you're trudging seems all uphill,
When the funds are low and the debts are high,
And you want to smile, but you have to sigh,
When care is pressing down a bit…
Rest if you must, but don't you quit.

Life is queer with its twists and turns,
As everyone of us sometimes learns,
And many a fellow turns about
When he might have won had he stuck it out,
Don't give up though the pace seems slow…
You may succeed with another blow.

It seems to a faint and faltering man;

Often the struggler has given up

When he might have captured the victor's cup;

And he learned too late when the night came down,

How close he was to the golden crown.

Success is failure turned inside out…

The silver tint of the clouds of doubt,

And you never can tell how close you are,

It may be near when it seems afar;

So stick to the fight when you're hardest hit…

It's when things seem worst that you mustn't quit.

Author Unknown

29. Here is one for all mankind to cherish. Or should I say….Mankind and Womankind so I can be politically correct.

The MAN IN THE GLASS teaches us the mind set of the difference between AVERAGE AND SPECIAL MIND SET.

THE MAN IN THE GLASS

When you've reached your goal in the world of sports
And you played the big game that day
Then go home to the mirror and look at yourself
And see what that man has to say.

For it isn't your coaches, your friends or your parents
Whose judgment upon you must pass
The man who's verdict counts most in your life
is the one looking back in the glass.

You may fool all of the world down the avenue of years
And get pats on the back as you pass
But your only rewards will be remorse and regret
If you've cheated the man in the glass.
AMEN!

Peter Dale Wimbrow Sr.

30. The Violinist

One day a famous violinist was approached by an admiring woman who said, "I would give my life to be able to play like you do." The violinist simply responded, "Madam......I did."

POSITIVE MIND SET…SPECIAL MIND SET know that only with a life long **commitment** to excellence…hard work and determination…can one become SPECIAL and NOT AVERAGE. We must use the example of the violinist in our everyday activities. NO EXCUSES. WE CAN DO IT. WE HAVE CONTROL. *Remember the concept of two types of life experiences…..experiences we have control over and those we have NO control over.*

In our development to make ourselves POSITIVE MIND SET…. …SPECIAL MIND SET, we must learn all of these concepts and lessons and most importantly, use them in our daily lives.

31. Work is great! Work is a great word!

Thomas Edison is credited with saying, "Opportunity is missed by most people because it is dressed in overalls and looks like work." You like it…...right? Great words by ole Tom! NEGATIVE MIND SET…AVERAGE MIND SET people think that WORK IS BAD.

Work….who likes work? Most people hate work! When actually work is great….work is fantastic…..work really means opportunity and NEGATIVE MIND SET...AVERAGE MIND SET people are always crying about they never get a chance....they never get an opportunity. Well, in this case, they better remember what ole Tom Edison had to say about it. DOMORE Baby......DOMORE......and you can become a HAVEMORE......you can become and think POSITIVE MIND SET...SPECIAL MIND SET. It is your choice. No one can stop you........except you....do you remember the..."The Man in the Glass"?

32. Work and Enthusiasm....
 ....great words of Paprus from Old Egyptian

Historical papers.

"If you can't get enthusiastic about your work, it's time to get

Alarmed......something is wrong.

No one keeps his enthusiasm automatically.

Enthusiasm must be nourished with new actions,

New aspirations, new efforts, new vision.

It is one's own fault if his enthusiasm is gone;

He has failed to feed it.

If you want to turn hours into minutes,

Renew your enthusiasm.

Great words from along time ago. A great example of POSITIVE MIND SET...SPECIAL MIND SET.

Paprus is saying….. "Put yourself on fire." You are in CONTROL. He is saying…..Don't point fingers at someone else…..we are in charge. Remember the ole Point Fingers joke. When we point a finger at anyone….three fingers actually point back to us which means WE are responsible.

33. Education

>There are two kinds of education.
>
>One teaches us to make a living.
>
>The other teaches us how to live.
>
>We need both types of education!
>
>Great words by Coach Gary Barnett

We can go to school….go to college and get a degree. Then we get a piece of paper. That piece of paper gets us an opportunity to possibly get a job. The so called education we got in our schools (actually just a beginning to our education) is nothing compared to the education we will receive living life.

NEGATIVE MIND SET...AVERAGE MIND SET may think that the degree we received makes us a SPECIAL person. WRONG! All the degree taught us was information.

We need reps in life to become SPECIAL. Reps mean......repetition….experience….experience…..experience.

Some NEGATIVE MIND SET…AVERAGE MIND SET thinking people think that because they got a college degree it makes them better or smarter than the person without a college degree. WRONG AGAIN! Many people without a college degree are smarter and wiser than the big shot with a college degree……because of life experiences…..REPS…. experience. Just like in sports….REPS….EXPERIENCE!

The REPS of life will include mistakes…..success….. pain……new learning and then again more mistakes and pain. Those human beings who learn to learn from their mistakes…their pain…..have a chance to become SPECIAL MIND SET. A school education is EASY. Life education is HARD.

In America, we live in a society that worships youth rather than older people. Older workers are in many instances thrown to the side. Bring in the youth, we are told. They have the energy. What a terrible mistake! When I coached in Germany for one year, my name was in the newspaper almost everyday. The newspaper would put my age next to my name every time my name was mentioned. I was amazed by this practice. I asked the President of our Club team about this practice. He stressed it was very important to mention my age. Age shows experience….wisdom. Wow! What a difference from America. In our country we hire young people who have less experience than the older people and end up making mistakes that the older people have already made. What a difference in mind set. Of course, in the U.S.A. many older people are not hired because of salary. Business can get two young people for the same salary as one older person. What a system!!!!!!!!!!!!! Just when a person knows what they are doing.....they get sent out to pasture. To my way of thinking....the age concept used in Germany was SPECIAL MIND SET.

34. Vince Lombardi and his Wisdom

Lombardi talked to business groups all over the country. He was one of the favorite speakers nation wide. I will mention a few of his WISDOMS which are characteristic of POSITIVE MIND SET...SPECIAL MIND SET.

Intensity.... "There is only one way to succeed at anything, and that is to give it everything you have. I do and I DEMAND that from my players."

Sacrifice..... "To achieve success, whatever the job we have, we must pay the price." .... Gotta be a DOMORE.

Belief...... "Confidence is contagious and so is *lack* of confidence, and a customer will recognize both. If you believe in yourself and have the courage, the determination, the dedication, the competitive drive and if you are willing to sacrifice the little things and *pay the price*, IT CAN BE DONE."

Commitment..... "The quality of a person's life is in direct proportion to their COMMITMENT to excellence, regardless of their chosen field of endeavor."

Character.... "In great attempts, it is glorious EVEN TO FAIL." Aw, ole Coach Lombardi was stressing to shoot high and if we fail we fail high....overcome the fear of failure and only by living in the ARENA do we really live.

Leadership....... "Leaders are NOT born....leaders are MADE." This means that anyone can learn to be a leader. Thus our expectations for everyone should be high.

Everyone can move from the NEGATIVE MIND SET... AVERAGE MIND SET to.......POSITIVE MIND SET... SPECIAL MIND SET.

Discipline..... "Once you learn to quit, it becomes a habit." Coach Lombardi was a preacher man......................a preacher of POSITIVE MIND SET...SPECIAL MIND SET.

35. Paul "Bear" Bryant.....great quotes which demonstrate POSITIVE MIND SET...SPECIAL MIND SET.

"What matters...is not the size of the dog in the fight that counts, but the fight in the dog that counts."

"In a crisis, don't hide behind anything or anybody. They're going to find you anyway."

"When you make a mistake....admit it; learn from it and damn well don't repeat it."

"age has nothing to do with it…..you can be out of touch at any age."

"The price of victory is high, but so are the rewards."

And finally, this very important POSITIVE MIND SET… SPECIAL MIND SET quality of Coach Bryant. He always carried a poem with him in his back pocket. The poem he cherished most read as follows;

This is the beginning of a new day.

God has given me this day to use as I will.

I can waste it or use it for good.

What I do today is very important because I am exchanging a day of my life for it.

When tomorrow comes, this day will be gone forever.

Leaving something in its place I have traded for it.

I want it to be a gain, not loss-good, not evil.

Success, not failure in order that I shall not forget the price I paid for it.

Is it any wonder why Coach Bryant was so successful? Nothing NEGATIVE or AVERAGE about this man.

36. "Pain is nothing more than weakness leaving the body…" -Daniel R.Evans

Here is a great example of "taking a negative and turning it into a positive" and " Do not allow the elements to affect your performance in a negative way." PAIN CAN BE USEFUL in the mind of the POSITIVE MIND SET….. SPECIAL MIND SET person. PAIN tells us that we have an opportunity to learn. "PAIN…..GOOD…..let me get those mistakes out of my system….out of my mind." This is very, very SPECIAL thinking. Once you learn to do this…. you become very, very STRONG…..very SPECIAL. Try it…..you'll like it!

37. The DO IT Principle…..

" Don't wait for your ship to come in…..swim out to meet it!" - John Mason

NEGATIVE MIND SET….AVERAGE MIND SET…. will just sit back and complain that they never get any luck….. they never get a chance. They live their life as a WISHMORE. POSITIVE MIND SET…SPECIAL MIND SET get after it….they just DO IT! What type of MIND SET are you?

38. How we respond!

Birth, growth, maturity, disability and death are realities of life. But……."Life is about HOW we respond to things. It is NOT about the hand we were dealt. It is about HOW we respond to the hand we were dealt."

This is a clear example of NEGATIVE vs. POSITIVE MIND SET…..AVERAGE vs. SPECIAL MIND SET.

39. Every man is the architect of his own future!

POSITIVE MIND SET...SPECIAL MIND SET folks understand this to be a fact. They understand *the things we have CONTROL over concept.*

NEGATIVE MIND SET...AVERAGE MIND SET folks blame circumstances for their situation. It is not their fault. They live in the world of EXCUSITIS.

40. John Wooten, the legendary basketball coach at UCLA said a great one;

"Be more concerned with your character than your reputation because it is your character which says what you really are all about, while your reputation is merely what others think you are."

NEGATIVE MIND SET...AVERAGE MIND SET folks are concerned more about their reputation than their character. They will do anything to succeed regardless of whether or not it is right or wrong. POSITIVE MIND SET...SPECIAL MIND SET folks are more concerned about doing the right thing. Their character is most important. They prefer to autograph their work with excellence. Remember the 90- 10 rule????? Along this same idea is what Socrates was credited with saying….."Give me beauty in the INWARD soul…. may the OUTWARD and INWARD of a man be at one." Socrates stressed that hopefully man develops himself so that his REPUTATION is the SAME as his CHARACTER.

41. Artistole was credited with saying......
    "We are what we repeatedly do."

In other words, if we are consistently in a NEGARIVE FORCE mode.....we will undoubtedly live in the AVERAGE MIND SET mode and be a 90 percenter (90-10 rule). If we consistently think and act positive is our daily relationship, we will live in the POSITIVE MIND SET mode and be a SPECIAL MIND SET person....a 10 percenter. "Yea team......!........That's what I wanna be....a 10 %er"

42. "Hold yourself to a higher standard
    than anybody else expects of you."....
    as said by Henry Ward Beecher.

WOW...WOW....WOW!

How many people do this?????? Only the few who dare to be a POSITIVE MIND SET.....SPECIAL MIND SET eagle! Again, I must refer to the poem.... "The Man in the Glass."

43. "Man's mind stretched to a new idea
    never goes back to its original dimensions."
    As stated by Oliver Wendell Holmes.

Ole Ollie gives us a tremendous attribute of POSITIVE MIND SET...SPECIAL MIND SET. Develop yourself to new horizons and you can never go back to where you were.

Years ago, I was speaking with an old man who was an immigrant from Italy. He spoke English with a heavy accent.

He was trying to give me some words of wisdom. This man had no formal education but he was over 80 years old and I knew that he lived longer than I and knew much more than I knew even though I just got my college degree. He lived life and graduated from the College of Living.

He said to me in his rough accent; (I will try to type the words as they sounded to me) He said……..."U must learn to developa u-self." I never forgot those words. I never forgot that old man. He gave me something very SPECIAL that day. A reminder that we as individuals MUST develop ourselves constantly. As Oliver Wendell Holmes said… "stretch your mind" and the old man said… "developa u-self." Thus creating that SPECIAL MIND SET.

44. John Wooten UCLA legendary basketball coach gives us another great one which I referred to earlier in this book.

"You can't live a perfect day without doing something for someone who will never be able to repay you."

WOW! How's that one for living a PERFECT DAY?

POSITIVE MIND SET…SPECIAL MIND SET people do things for people without holding them hostage to the concept….."you owe me… because of what I did for you." The truth is that people do not owe us anything when we do something for them. We did something for them because we wanted to do so. Period. We did it for ourselves FIRST. Because we WANTED to. It made us feel good about ourselves.

NEGATIVE MIND SET…AVERAGE MIND SET believes……"you owe me." They keep a checklist of the things they DID for you and when the time is right, they come to you for payment of the things they DID for you. They always have STRINGS ATTACHED to whatever they do.

45. "Great leaders are rarely REALISTIC….. by other people's standards."

Again…..a great difference between AVERAGE and SPECIAL MIND SET thinking. Sometimes we hear people say; "Those are not REALISTIC goals." Yea……by who's standards?

We need to dream of the Impossible! Only then do we have a chance to reach the moon. Remember what Albert Einstein said….. "Imagination is more important than intelligence." We have to dream of UN-REALISTIC goals if we are to be SPECIAL and NOT AVERAGE MIND SET.

46. *"Achievers do not see a problem as permanent…..while those that do not achieve see a problem as permanent."*

POSITIVE MIND SET…SPECIAL MIND SET never see a problem as permanent. They love to take problems and change them into challenges. They love being PROBLEM SOLVERS. They know that this is how one builds STRENGTH. WEAKNESS….NEGATIVE MIND SET…AVERAGE MIND SET…..see problems as being permanent. "Problems.....oh I have problems." They use words like "can't". Do you remember what can't means?

Do you remember the name Friday in the story Robinson Crusoe which was written by Daniel Dufoe? Well, Dufoe wrote the story and he had Friday saying the following;

"Living life is not important.....How you live life is important."
"To die is not important.....How you die is important."

I love it. Great, Great words by Dufoe. Thanks Dan for giving us a great example of POSITIVE MIND SET...SPECIAL MIND SET.

47. This is an old one but worth using over and over again. I got this one

from my ole coaching buddy Dominick Bramante.

Thoughts

Watch your thoughts
For they become words
Choose your words
For they become actions
Understand your actions
For they become habits
Study your habits
For they become your character
Develop your character
For it becomes your destiny!

Jewish Rabbi Hillel the Elder

POSITIVE MIND SET…SPECIAL MIND SET is always trying to make themselves better. They know that their THOUGHTS become *them*.

48. Anthony Robbins gives us this thought;

"The secret of success is learning how to use PAIN and PLEASURE instead of having PAIN and PLEASURE use us. If we do this, we are in control of our life. If we don't, then life controls us. "

A great example of the concept of Two Types of Life Experiences….those we have CONTROL over and those we have NO CONTROL over. POSITIVE MIND SET…SPECIAL MIND SET strives to make the decisions that they have CONTROL over. They understand that experiences they have NO CONTROL over must not destroy them mentally,if the results are not successful.

49. Pay the Price or Else….

"you pay the price to get smarter."
"you pay the price to get better."
"you pay the price to succeed."

"YOU PAY THE PRICE TO STAY THE SAME."

Author Unknow

In order to be a 10 percenter….in order to be a POSITIVE MIND SET…SPECIAL MIND SET…..in order to be a HAVEMORE FAMILY member………..you have to be a DOMORE…..you must INVEST greatly……..you must increase your commitment…….you must not accept mediocrity. YOU MUST PAY THE PRICE. Just do it! You will love it! Living in the POSITIVE MIND SET… SPECIAL MIND SET is a wonderful experience. Once you live in this POSITIVE- SPECIAL MIND SET world you will never want to go back to the NEGATIVE MIND SET…AVERAGE MIND SET world. As Oliver Wendell Holmes said…."Once you stretch your MIND, you can never go back to the old MIND SET."

50. The English Statesman Francis Bacon stated;

"A wise man will MAKE more opportunities than he FINDS."

Certainly NOT the mind set of a NEGATIVE MIND SET…AVERAGE MIND SET person. MAKE your opportunity……don't LOOK for it. Be a DOMORE!

51. "It is necessary for us to learn from other's mistakes. We will not live long enough to make them all ourselves."

Great words of SPECIAL thinking by the distinguished Admiral Hyman Rickover, United States Navy. Learn by observing. Watch others. Learn from FAILURE. Learn from

PAIN. Learn not only from our own FAILURE and PAIN, but from the FAILURE and PAIN of others.

This is SPECIAL thinking.

52. General George Patton was quoted; "Wars are lost in the MIND before they are lost on the ground."

Ole George was talking about MIND SET long before I did. Thus, I learned in coaching football, I was going to have to coach the MIND SET of my players FIRST before we ever tried to play the game of football.

53. "The diamond cannot be polished without FRICTION, nor man perfected without TRIALS AND tribulations.'

This Old Chinese proverb shows us that the ancient Chinese were well aware of the fact that people only develop themselves by overcoming PAIN….overcoming CHALLENGES(Problems)…..only by becoming a DOMORE…..only by becoming a PROBLEM SOLVER. The ancient Chinese knew that in order for man to be perfected, he would have to learn to overcome all the failure and frustrations that go into living life. The Chinese learned to be VERY…… POSITIVE MIND SET…SPECIAL MIND SET.

54. George Bernard Shaw said a great one.

Likes and Dislikes

Forget about likes and dislikes. They are of no consequences. Just do what must be done. This may not be happiness, but it is GREATNESS.
Sooooooooo….if you wanna be SPECIAL MIND SET… JUST DO IT! Don't worry about LIKING it!

55. Discipline is NOT what you do to someone….. Discipline is what you do FOR someone.

NEGATIVE MIND SET…AVERAGE MIND SET…may use discipline to *punish* someone. They may use discipline because of anger towards that person. POSITIVE MIND SET…SPECIAL MIND SET will use discipline because they feel the person receiving the discipline needs to learn that we all have to be held accountable for what we do. If the person getting disciplined, doesn't learn from this NEGATIVE type of experience, then the discipline was for NOTHING. It was worthless!

56. General Colin Powell said; "If you are going to achieve excellence in BIG things, you have to develop the habit in LITTLE matters. Excellence is not an exception, it is a prevailing attitude."

General Powell was stressing that in order to have excellence, we have to pay attention to detail…the small things. This is another characteristic of POSITIVE MIND SET…

SPECIAL MIND SET. We have to autograph our work with excellence in all things….even the small things….in every detail. General Powell sounds a lot like Coach Vince Lombardi when Coach said, "Winning attitude is NOT a sometime thing…..winning attitude *is an all the time thing.*"

57. The writer Arthur C. Clarke wrote……"The only way to discover the limits of the possible is to go beyond them into the impossible."

WOW! Overcoming the FEAR OF FAILURE and going into the world of the POSITIVE MIND SET…SPECIAL MIND SET. Being a DREAMER. Never using the word…. CAN'T.

58. President John F. Kennedy reminded us during one of his speeches that the word CRISIS is composed of two characters.

One represents DANGER….the other represents OPPORTUNITY.

NEGATIVE MIND SET…AVERAGE MIND SET thinking will perceive the word CRISIS to be a bad word. Something we want to avoid. POSITIVE MIND SET…SPECIAL MIND SET see the word CRISIS as an "opportunity" to overcome a "danger." A challenge. A chance to be a "problem solver." A chance to be SPECIAL.

I hope you enjoyed these lessons that I use in my Football Bible. They have been very good to me in the past. They all have great meaning and are an inspiration to me every time I read them. I hope they do the same for you. Notice that I repeated several thoughts and stories many times. This was necessary to accomplish the goal of REPS! REPS…..REPS……over and over and over again…..these concepts have to be drilled into your head and used on a daily basis.

Good Luck World…….STAY POSITIVE………..BE SPECIAL Don't cheat our CREATOR!!!!!!!!

Chapter 14
Developing a Simple program

Now it's time to talk about developing and using a SIMPLE program that you can use for yourself or for other members of your family, such as your children.

Step 1-

Step 1 was the first reading of this book. NOW YOU NEED REPS. Just like an athlete. You need REPS!

Step-2

Step 2 is going back and giving yourself Fifteen Minutes a Day to Read one chapter or parts of one chapter once AGAIN.

You need REPS to get to the point where the concepts get into your head. Remember....you have to use the same words. Do not change the words. If you were learning to sing a song, you would not change the words of the song. *Don't change the words of the Concepts.*

Step-3

The next day…..read the same passage that you read yesterday. You need REPS in what you read. Each day you read the same information, you will pick up on new thoughts. You will remember the concepts mentioned with additional reps. To remember the concept of EXCUSITIS is easy, since it is only one word.

To remember the concept….."Take a negative and turn it into a positive" is longer….more words…..so you need reps to remember the exact words.

Step-4

Continue working though the book. Repeating information…getting REPS. By now, you are thinking of your own life experiences and you are evaluating these experiences.

Do they fall into NEGATIVE MIND SET? POSITIVE MIND SET? Do they fall into the 90-10 rule? Etc…etc. Evaluate your own behavior. Was it NEGATIVE or POSITIVE MIND SET? Have some FUN! Sit down with your spouse or children and talk about things you all did and how you acted. Evaluate these acts of behavior.

Consider the following; Was the behavior;
- weakness or strength
- Negative or Positive FORCE
- Negative or Positive MIND SET
- Average or Special MIND SET
- 90 % or 10% as in the 90-10 Rule
- Was EXCUSITIS used?
- Did the person OVERCOME THE FEAR OF FALIURE?
- Did the person TAKE A NEGATIVE AND TURN IT INTO A POSITIVE?
- Did the person go under the water…using the concept The Iceberg Theory Of Thinking.
- Was the person being a Wishmore? Stress the 3 Major Families of the World.
- Did the person get trapped into using Generalities?
- Did the person insist on trying to HAVE THEIR OWN WAY?
- Did the person learn TO GIVE CONTROL TO GET CONTROL?
- Was wrong Terminology used to cause wrong Perception?
- Did the person use PUSH PEOPLE UP?
- Did the person use the expression HATE?
- Did the person try to DEFUSE a situation?
- Did the person show Enthusiasm? Did the person GET EXCITED?
 Did they PUT THEMSELVES ON FIRE?
- Did the person try to SELL and NOT TELL?
- Did the person use the concept….DON'T WORRY ABOUT THE THINGS
 WE HAVE NO CONTROL OF?

-Did the person have THICK SKIN….or….THIN SKIN?
-Did the person TAKE IT PERSONAL?
-How did the person react to criticism?
-How did the person react to a MISTAKE? Do they understand the Concept….DECISIONS.
-Does the person understand when someone is allowing themselves to walk with the Devil?
-Did the person give commitment?
-Did the person develop or give TRUST?
-Did the person really pay the price in the attempt to be successful?
 Do they understand that some people THINK THAT SMALL IS BIG?
-Did the person fall into the NEGATIVE Trap of Expectations.

This interaction with other people may seem hard to do at the beginning, but once you gain self-confidence and *learn to not fear failure*, it will become easy to interact with others and discuss these concepts.

Have some FUN!   Try it!   You will like it! And you will learn!

Step-5

Continue through the book. After you complete the book, read it once again. You will NEVER GET ENOUGH REPS!

Good Luck and have some FUN!